Survival Mom's No Worries Guide

Emergency Evacuations:
Get Out Fast When It Matters Most!

By Lisa Bedford

EMERGENCY EVACUATIONS

Copyright © 2015 Lisa Bedford All rights reserved, including the right to copy, reproduce and distribute this book, or portions thereof, in any form. The Survival Mom.
ISBN: 1942533020
ISBN-13: 978-1-942533-02-3

LISA BEDFORD

Thanks so much for purchasing this book. I hope it is a great help to you and your loved ones.

As a special gift, I've recorded a 30-minute webinar that adds even more helpful information for your evacuation plans,
"7 Lessons From Hurricane Katrina."

To access this free webinar, visit
http://thesurvivalmom.com/evacwebinar
Thanks again for your purchase!

EMERGENCY EVACUATIONS

LISA BEDFORD

An Introduction

Moms worry about many things, from the mundane to the truly scary. We worry about the expectations of others, how to get our kids to eat healthy snacks, and whether or not we should be concerned about the latest news headlines.

Survival Moms worry, too, but we know that worrying doesn't change anything, nor does it prepare us if things go wildly wrong. So, we take charge. We brainstorm, research, make lists, and find ways to make our homes and families ready for everyday emergencies and even worst case scenarios.

One emergency that few households are prepared for is an emergency evacuation. Whether it's a sudden house fire, rising flood waters, or a tornado that devastates a town, we want to be ready to grab the most essential items, kids and pets, especially, and get out of danger's way.

Survival Mom's No Worries Guide to Emergency Evacuations will provide you with the tools, strategies, and motivation to put everything in place should you need to evacuate your home in a crisis. You'll learn the difference between an **urgent** evacuation and a **planned** evacuation, and how to prepare for both. You'll have convenient lists for emergency kits that cover babies, pets, and even elderly loved ones. Also in this book, you'll find strategies for getting out of the house quickly and planning the best

EMERGENCY EVACUATIONS

routes to safety.

Preparedness brings peace of mind and a whole lot less to worry about!

Lisa Bedford
The Survival Mom
October 8, 2015

LISA BEDFORD

Table of Contents

An Introduction 5
Table of Contents 7
Evacuations: Chaotic. Confusing. Terrifying......................11
    An emergency evacuation vs. bugging out 11
    Two types of evacuations 12
    Case study: a real-life urgent evacuation. 16
When is it time to leave? 21
    Key word: imminent 22
    Hunkering down may not be the best choice 23
    Staying informed to make an informed decision 23
    What if everyone isn't all together? 24
    Getting the kids back home 25
Emergency kits, packed & ready 29
    Standard supplies for an emergency kit 30
    Grab-n-Go Binder (vital documents) 34
    Does it have to be a backpack? 38
    Special kits for special family members..............................40
    Packing water 47
    Comfort items for stressful times..48

EMERGENCY EVACUATIONS

Case Study: Evacuating a special needs loved one 49
What can you absolutely, positively not leave behind? 51
The last minute packing list 53
The All-Important Staging Area 58
Think outside the box when it comes to evacuation destinations 60
    Campgrounds 60
    Urban camping 61
    Camping on friends' property 61
    Mobile home park 62
    Hotels 62
    Timeshares 62
    Airbnb 62
    Youth hostels 63
    Stay with friends of friends 63
    Non-government shelters 63
    Learn from the homeless 65
    Staying sane under (very) trying circumstances! 66
    Final considerations 69
Hitting the road 71
    Multiple, planned routes 71
    Route considerations 72
    Practice driving your routes 75
    Your getaway vehicle: not just for bank robbers! 76
    Equip your vehicle for emergencies 78
    Evacuation on foot 80

Getting ready to leave: the final moments 84
    A word about insurance 86
    Rehearsals: practice makes perfect 87
    Evacuation to-do list 89
    Case study: Hurricane evacuations 90
Your mindset really matters 93
    Human "wiring" 94
    Muscle memory 94
    Anxiety 95
    Case study: Mental preparation 97
Eventually, you'll return home 99
    When you return 99
    Case study: a real-life flood survivor 100
Prepare more, panic less 103
Acknowledgements 105
Appendixes 107
Evacuation supplies checklist 109
    Sustenance 109
    Sanitation supplies 110
    Sanity 110
    Security 111
    Survival 111
Evacuation to-do list 113
    Optional: based on situation & weather conditions 113
    Final Actions 114
Last-minute packing list 115

EMERGENCY EVACUATIONS

Afterword 119
About the author 120
Also by Lisa Bedford 121
  Forthcoming: 122
Contact the author. 124

LISA BEDFORD

Evacuations: Chaotic. Confusing. Terrifying.

An all-too familiar scene that accompanies disasters and major crises of all kinds is a crowd of bewildered and desperate people – men, women, and children – carrying random suitcases, backpacks, and trash bags loaded with their only remaining belongings.

These refugees, for that is what they are, have fled an event that became so dangerous they feared for their lives and entered a scenario requiring them to depend on the kindness and generosity of strangers, which itself is a risk.

Escaping danger wearing only the clothes on your back and grabbing random items as you rush out the door is the worst possible way to "do" an evacuation! Even in the face of a house fire or oncoming tornado, preplanning and preparation make all the difference in the world for getting out quickly and safely.

This guide will help you predict potential threats to your home and family and create a customized plan for an emergency evacuation.

An emergency evacuation vs. bugging out

If you're familiar with the prepper world, you know that no topic is more popular than bugging out. Preppers love to debate and discuss their bug out routes, bug out locations, contents of their bug out bags, and even which vehicle is the best for, you guessed it, bugging out!

In these discussions, and in countless blog articles and books, bugging out involves hitting the road and leaving home forever in the face of a worst case scenario such as an economic or societal collapse. For sure, an EMP (electro-magnetic pulse) or the eruption of the Yellowstone caldera would necessitate evacuating far away and for good. None of these scenarios are out of the question, and it's very possible that certain SHTF events might necessitate extreme decisions and actions. However, mundane events that would, nevertheless, require heading to a safer place are far more likely. So mundane are these events that the most popular survival websites barely give them a mention!

The truth is that most evacuations become necessary due to everyday emergencies, and that is the topic of this *No Worries Guide*.

Two types of evacuations

A house fire or a chemical spill can cause us to race out of the house with moments to spare. Other types of disasters, however, give us enough advance warning with hours, perhaps even days, to prepare.

Whether a future evacuation becomes necessary due to an everyday emergency or a worst case scenario, you need to have plans and preps in place for both. Depending on what sort of emergency you face, your evacuation will be either **urgent** or **planned.** You'll read about both types on the next few pages and learn how to begin putting plans in place for each.

Urgent evacuation

It's the middle of the night and the smell of smoke awakes you to a house fire. There is no time to mosey from room to room searching for important documents and making several trips to and from your car in order to pack more supplies. There is no time at all to do anything other than react. You must just get out! In these cases, it is doubtful there will be time to do much else. If you pause to gather pets, supplies, valuables, and documents, you are more likely to endanger yourself and your loved ones.

In the case of a widespread, sudden emergency, scrambling at the last minute, deciding what to take and what to leave behind, will take precious minutes you don't have. It also increases the chance that you'll run into major traffic issues as panicked people also try to get away from harm.

Possible scenarios that may necessitate an urgent evacuation:

- Avalanche
- Earthquake
- Explosion
- Chemical spill nearby
- Landslide
- Mudslide
- Floods
- Nuclear event
- Riots
- Terrorist attack
- Tornadoes
- Tsunami

In the case of an urgent evacuation, it's doubly important

EMERGENCY EVACUATIONS

to be prepared since you will be managing your own fears as well as those of your loved ones. Even pets will react to your strong emotions. At times like this, your brain will kick in by sending not-so-helpful messages that instruct you to flee, fight, or freeze. None of those options are very helpful at this moment, but by having an evacuation routine in place, routes planned, and emergency kits ready to go, you'll have a better chance of fighting back against those emotions and brain messages. If you've rehearsed the evacuation in a family drill, you'll be even better prepared to survive.

<u>Be prepared: Grab and run!</u>

Since you never know when you may have to run from home in the middle of the night, it's smart to have just a few key items in a small bag, something similar to a zippered cosmetic bag or a nylon drawstring backpack, kept in your bedside table or hanging on a bedpost. This isn't your main emergency kit or bug out bag, but is meant to hold just a few essentials in case that's all you have time to grab.

That bag could contain:

- A small but powerful LED flashlight
- A whistle (helpful if a tornado or powerful earthquake leaves you trapped in your home).
- Spare pair of eyeglasses and/or contact lenses
- A multi-tool with a good blade
- Hand and foot warmers if you live in a cold climate
- A pair of very warm (possibly wool) socks
- Cash
- A photo ID

Planned evacuation

The second type of evacuation to consider and prepare for is a planned evacuation. An example of this is when news of a hurricane begins to dominate the attention of the media.

Thanks to modern technology, meteorologists can predict with a fair degree of accuracy when and where these will make landfall. You may have days to plan for your evacuation before it occurs. Ideally, you will already have your emergency kits prepped and ready to go, with appropriate clothing and food rations for each person. Everyone knows what he or she is responsible for. With these basic things out of the way, you are free to do additional planning that will make your time away from home go more smoothly.

Besides a hurricane, there are other possible scenarios that may necessitate a planned evacuation:

- Earthquake – Your home may be reparable and safe to enter, but not habitable. Simply having a water main break may necessitate leaving your home.
- Hurricane
- Epidemic or pandemic
- Rising floodwaters
- "Storm of the Century" — Blizzard or otherwise, you may want to get out to avoid the worst.
- Volcanic eruption — Volcanoes usually give some warning before erupting, but once they blow, time's up.
- Wildfires in the area – These can abruptly change direction. Stay safe and be prepared to flee.

Ironically, in spite of having time to plan, evaluate routes, and double check all your preparations, planned evacuations may not go smoothly due to factors beyond your control. It may be difficult to persuade family members that now is the time to go. The weather and road conditions may not cooperate and authorities, including law enforcement, may have made decisions that affect your route and ability to move quickly.

One Survival Mom reader, Gille, told me about a hurricane evacuation in which she and her family traveled 24 hours to reach a destination that was just 4 hours away. At one point they stopped at a gas station to sleep and woke to armed police limiting the amount of gasoline that could be purchased by customers — one gallon per person!

As with any type of emergency evacuation, make your plans, stay informed, be ready to move when it becomes necessary, but be prepared to make last minute adjustments. The ability to adapt quickly is key to survival.

> **TIP:** Throughout this book and in the Appendix are several checklists for your use. You can make copies of those in the Appendix or download them.
>
> http://thesurvivalmom.com/downloadable-resources

Case study: a real-life urgent evacuation.

Marilyn, a Texas mom and registered nurse, told me the story of how a house fire forced her family to evacuate late one night.

"Around 11:30 one winter night, my spouse and I were watching TV in bed with our door closed. Our 18 year old son was in the living room on the computer and in our basement lived a single gent who was renting that space.

My husband and I started smelling something like burned toast, and I opened the bedroom door to ask my son what he was cooking/burning. As I opened the bedroom door, I heard him yelling that smoke was coming out the furnace vents. At the same time, I heard the basement tenant banging around downstairs, knocking over furniture. I yelled at my son that the house was on fire and to get out.

It was at this point that our prior planning and preparedness for just this type of event helped but still, mistakes were made, as you'll see.

We have been foster parents for delinquent teens, and because of this, we were required to have certain safety procedures in place. Bedrooms doors were always closed when occupied, and fire drill plans were framed and hung by bedroom doors. From time to time, we even had actual drills. Our written plans included instructions to check the bedroom doorknob for heat before opening and to not open it if the room was already smoky or the door was hot. We also had a prearranged meeting spot outside so we could make sure that each person was safe. As part of our fire safety plans, everyone was always told to not wait around inside the house or look around for things to "rescue". We made sure that everyone knew to climb out of a window if a doorway led into an unsafe, smoke-filled area.

The night of our house fire, I first opened our bedroom door and for just a few seconds, I couldn't believe what I saw. Yes, the house was on fire and what happened next, happened within just a couple of panic-filled minutes!

Before going to sleep at night, I've always put our 3 dogs in their kennels. On this particular night, only one was in his kennel, and the other 2 were loose in our bedroom. Our cat was allowed to roam the house. As soon as I opened the bedroom door to check on the smell of smoke, the 2 loose dogs ran to the side door as they were used to going out to the yard that way. My spouse, without checking, opened the side door. Later, I learned that smoke was billowing out from under that door and the two dogs were killed, most likely immediately, by the heat and smoke. It was a very sad loss.

My husband, son, and I ran out the front door in our pajamas and into a snowy, frigid night. Because one toy poodle was in his kennel, we were able to grab him as we raced to safety. My son was able to go back to the front door and grab coats, shoes and, luckily, our wallets and my purse. They were all hanging on hooks by the front door. From just those few, brief seconds in the smoke-filled house, however, my son experienced a significant smoke inhalation injury.

Once all three of us were outside, my son dialed 911. This all occurred in a matter of just two or three minutes from when we first smelled smoke. It happened so fast!

We basically lost everything in this fire. The gentleman who was living in the basement died. He had fallen asleep smoking.

Looking back, we did a lot of things right in spite of the tragic outcome of this event. We had planned for a potential house fire, even if those plans weren't executed perfectly. Having our coats, wallets, and shoes by our main exit point, the front door, worked out great, and we needed all those items! The money and debit/credit cards in our wallets allowed us to drive to a hotel, pay for a room, and buy food and other necessities during the days initially following the fire. Keeping our dogs in kennels at night is something I still do, both for their safety and my comfort. Our established meeting place allowed us to quickly confirm that everyone was okay and what each person had done, e.g. call 911, evacuate the kenneled dog, etc. It also gave us a primary goal to focus on: get to that meeting place! It was a huge relief to know that we were all safe.

The mistakes that we made included not having all the dogs kenneled earlier. I opened the bedroom door without thinking. I honestly did not initially consider a fire, but my biggest mistake was not accurately assessing and understanding family members' strengths and limitations. My son did everything he was trained to do. My husband, not so much. As a RN, I knew panic often sets in when there's an emergency, and this was a huge one! I'm trained to assess and give firm direction to those who cannot function, but when I needed to put that training to use with my own family members, I failed to remember this danger or to recognize it. Because of that, I was unable to give firm directions, which may have helped us get out more quickly, stopped our dogs from exiting a very dangerous doorway, or possibly salvaged more of our belongings at the last minute.

In our panic mode we forgot to assess doorknobs for heat and smoke. We lost two dogs and a cat and if I hadn't intervened quickly, we would have been dealing with the death of my husband, who was standing directly in front of a mass of fire and smoke. I now realize, more than ever, that not everyone can handle major crises like this one. If you recognize signs of that tendency before something happens, you can provide specific, verbal directions and, potentially, avoid some disasters.

In hindsight we came out okay. Insurance covered a bit, enough to help us buy the most important necessities for re-establishing a household, but the money wasn't nearly enough. Smoke damage is terrible and almost impossible to get out of any belongings.

My main regret is that I didn't accurately assess the people I lived with to have an idea of how they might react under intense pressure. This would hold true in any emergency, and is something I definitely do much better now!"

> **Tip:** Marilyn's tip for working with people unable to cope in a crisis is to give them a single, simple direction, such as, "Go outside and wait for the ambulance," or "Bring me the first aid kit." This gets the traumatized person away from the immediate situation, gives them something simple on which to focus, and provides time to calm down and, hopefully, begin to think clearly again.

LISA BEDFORD

When is it time to leave?

This really is the $40,000 question, isn't it? Sometimes it's painfully obvious that it's time to leave, such as when the walls of your home begin collapsing after an earthquake. Other times, it's hard to tell when to make the call.

Unless your emergency is one that requires racing out of the house with nothing more than the clothes on your back, you'll likely have time to consider whether it's smarter to stay put and hunker down or leave. The answer to this question isn't as clear cut as it may seem.

I've heard it said that once the authorities give the word to evacuate, it's already too late. Like hundreds of others, perhaps hundreds of thousands of others, you've waited for the official go-ahead and now you'll be fighting everyone else for the few routes available that will take you away from the danger zone.

While it's vital to pay attention to official sources, it's just as important to rely on your own eyes, ears, and common sense to know when it's time to leave or whether the safest choice is to stay.

At times like these, pay attention to the neighborhood or workplace rumor mill. I'm a fan of getting news from alternate sources and often news leaks from official sources can be helpful. Keep in mind that your safety and that of your loved ones will be determined by the decisions and actions you take and evaluate the sources carefully. Be careful about making decisions based on something that a friend of a friend reports.

Once you leave home, especially in a dire emergency, you've become just another refugee. You've probably seen news footage of desperate refugees from around the world, carrying pillow cases and plastic trash bags filled with the only belongings they could grab at the last minute. If these refugees are lucky, their path will take them to a tent city set up by emergency relief workers. In many cases, though, their trail ends in starvation, injury, and often, violence and death.

It may sound far-fetched that this could happen to you, but Hurricane Katrina didn't exactly bring out the best in many people, and those who were most affected were the ones who didn't leave their homes in time and ended up relying on others for even the most basic supplies, such as water and toilet facilities.

Key word: imminent

The key factor in knowing when it's time to leave is the word "imminent". Are you and your loved ones in imminent danger? A household fire presents an imminent danger, but a wildfire burning up acres of forest land 50 miles away isn't quite an imminent threat and may never become one.

An earthquake or tornado that leaves your home severely damaged requires a quick evacuation because it no longer is a safe refuge. There's imminent danger if you stay put because the structure itself presents serious danger.

When evaluating the need to evacuate, ask, "Is the threat imminent?" Err on the side of safety by overestimating the level of imminent danger in order to give yourself a margin of time to make decisions, prepare, and leave.

Hunkering down may not be the best choice

If you decide to stay at home and not evacuate after all, you are gambling that you'll be able to get out at some point in the future. A danger may not be imminent <u>now</u> but that could change, and by the time you make the decision to hit the road, you could very well find yourself in the midst of a horde of people who also postponed their departure, or trapped by damaged roads, destroyed bridges, and impassable highways.

Staying home also presents the possibility, however remote, that there will be food, gasoline, and supply shortages; a long-term power outage to endure; and even a lack of fresh water and operating sewer systems. If you have septic and / or well systems, a power outage means those won't work, either.

On the other hand, at home you're in familiar surroundings with neighbors and loved ones who, hopefully, will be willing to join with you in sharing resources and protecting property. All your stored gear and food will be in one place, and you know the lay of the land. If you have kids, remaining in their own home, as long as it's safe to do so, will surely be less traumatic.

Staying informed to make an informed decision

Information is going to be your most important ally in the first moments, hours, and days of an emergency. If you or your kids have a smartphone or tablet, install apps that provide alerts for inclement weather, tornadoes, earthquakes, and hurricanes. If, during your evacuation route, you must pass through or near a major metropolitan area, a traffic-tracking app would also be helpful, as well as one that helps you find gas stations. If you have a GPS that tracks this information, don't forget to keep the maps updated and bring it along.

The Red Cross makes several excellent emergency apps. Even FEMA has a phone app that provides weather alerts, tips for building an emergency kit, and more. If you have a "not-so-smart phone," be sure you are familiar with your local AM news radio station. Having a HAM radio license and operating radios would be exceedingly helpful, as well. Very often, it's the amateur radio operators who are communicating first following a major disaster.

What if everyone isn't all together?

Be prepared for the eventuality that your family may be separated during the time when an urgent evacuation is necessary – Dad at work, Mom at home with the little ones, older kids away at school. Have a plan in place that enables you to contact your family members, whether it is a family tracker app, such as Life360, a spare set of walkie-talkies in the car (with spare batteries), or some other method.

At this point, communication becomes most vital. In the case of an urgent evacuation, it will be enough to make a quick phone call or send a text to family members letting them know you are safe.

In a planned evacuation, though, everyone must stay up to date with the latest news and weather and have a pre-determined point at which the evacuation will move forward.

It can take days for a hurricane to pose a danger, as they

often linger hundreds of miles off shore, making up their minds as to which direction they'll travel. It wouldn't make any sense to pack up the kids, dogs, and ice chest when the hurricane is still a Category 2 in the middle of the Atlantic.

Instead, set triggers to help you decide when your family will begin loading up the car and making final preparations to leave. In the case of a hurricane, those might be when the storm's trajectory places your home directly in its path and you live within the evacuation boundaries.

If everyone knows those triggers, they can track them, no matter where they happen to be, so they will know when it's time to head home.

This takes the wild guesswork out of a situation in which nerves are becoming more frayed by the hour and keeps everyone on the same well-informed page.

Getting the kids back home

Ask your child's school teacher and administrators what their plan is for the types of natural disasters that are most likely in your area. Those plans should be available on the school's website or in a Parent Handbook.

If your plan is to rush to your child's classroom and grab her, your visit may not be a welcome one. A crowd of parents all intent on doing the same thing is a school administrator's nightmare and an unauthorized person grabbing a child is entirely possible.

In a worst case scenario where you absolutely must get your child, first approach the school office and attempt to go through the official, established steps of checking your child out. Be prepared to show your ID and sign them out

EMERGENCY EVACUATIONS

just like you would any other day.

If you can't personally pick them up, be sure the person you send in your place has both their photo ID and a signed, dated note from you that gives that specific person authorization to pick up your child on that day. Be sure to include the name of your child's teacher as well as the child's name to help speed the process along. If your school has a specific form for this, use it. The easier you make things on the office staff, the faster you will get your child home.

However, the very first person you should talk with about getting your child home safely in an emergency is the child herself. In the chaos and aftermath of a tornado, earthquake, or long-term power outage, the chance that she could go home with a friend, attempt to walk home on their own, or panic and run away is fairly likely.

Talk with your kids and make sure they know the plan. If you are going to pick them up, be sure they know that you will do everything you can to pick them up and they should remain at the school until you, or someone you send, gets there. If they have a close friend near the school and you are comfortable with them going home with that person, you can call or email the change to their teacher and the office on that day, but it might be missed in the hubbub so make sure your child knows to listen for it.

Here's one possible game plan for a conversation like this one:

1. Talk to your kids about what types of emergencies might occur that are common to your area. Discuss how your family has weathered such events before and what you've done to keep the family safe.
2. Review with them the official school routine for

checking kids out of school.
3. If your kids have cell phones, that phone is an important lifeline to you in case of an emergency. If the school rule is that cell phones cannot be used during school hours, let your child know that in the case of one of the emergencies you discussed, they should tell their teacher that you'll be contacting them. It would be a good idea for you to email the teacher as well to give them a heads-up.

   At the very least, they should have their phone powered on with the ringer off. Remind them to charge their phone at night so it has full power when they go to school. This way, they will still be able to receive text messages from you.
4. If your child doesn't normally carry a cell phone, an inexpensive "disposable" cell phone could be a good investment.

By the way, additional phones can be added to a family's cell phone plan for a few dollars each month. I know that kids can misuse cell phones but in an emergency, nothing beats having that line of communication to the little ones in your life.

Our kids have had their own cell phones since they were 10 and 11 years old. On one occasion, my daughter was able to alert me to an extreme medical emergency she was experiencing, so I'm a fan of kids and the smart use of cell phones.

A good option to the cell phone is a set of two-way radios. These can be kept in a backpack and turned on only when needed. Add a set of spare batteries and it's an inexpensive way to stay in touch.

For sure, don't be shy about asking your child's teacher

about emergency plans and volunteer to participate in helping the students and school be more secure and prepared.

> **TIP:** Have kids away at college? They, too, should have an emergency kit and know how to utilize every item it contains. Should they ever need to evacuate their campus, first find out if an official plan is in place and keep that information in mind. However, controlling the actions of thousands of young adults is something no college or university can completely put into place, so your student should also have a plan of his own.
>
> Along with a well-equipped kit, that might include a laminated map marked with multiple directions leading to safe places, a couple hundred dollars in small bills to pay for transportation, food, and lodging. Encourage your student to find others headed the same direction and travel together since there's usually safety in numbers.

LISA BEDFORD

Emergency kits, packed & ready

We preppers love a good emergency kit. Whether you call it a *72 hour kit*, a *Bug-Out-Bag*, or a *Run Bucket*, you should have one for each member of your family.

What is an emergency kit? It's a collection of basic supplies that will support you for at least three days, preferably more, while you are away from home and have no other means of support. FEMA has repeatedly said that it often takes at least 72 hours before they are ready to begin services and administer relief to disaster zones. FEMA is neither the most efficient nor most reliable source of assistance, and during those first few days, you should plan to be completely on your own. You will need food, water, and other vital supplies, especially if you are away from home.

A kit is an effective way to have all those vital supplies in one place, rather than scattered around the house.

It's possible to purchase these kits pre-made, and that is what most people do. If you do buy a pre-made kit, go through it regularly to become familiar with the contents, and be sure to add items that are unique to your needs.

One of the biggest drawbacks to most of the ready-made kits is the lack of quality found in many of the supplies. There's also the assumption that the new owner of the kit will know exactly how to utilize each item in it. When you really, truly need an item and your life depends on it, quality counts for more than anything else, so double check each item and make sure it will do its job when it matters most and that you have some skill in putting it to use.

As easy as it might be to fork over the money for a kit that's ready to go, I recommend assembling your own from scratch. When you put your own kit together, you can easily seek out the items that are most suitable for your use and many you probably have around the house already.

Standard supplies for an emergency kit

I like to refer to The 5 S's when it comes to packing an emergency kit of any kind. Every kit should contain items vital to these 5 categories:

1. Sanitation
2. Sustenance
3. Survival
4. Safety
5. Sanity

You will need supplies in each of these and they cover the gamut from items that will help you stay calm throughout a crisis to hard-core survival supplies, such as paracord and a good knife.

When it comes to sustenance, an emergency kit should contain enough food to keep you and everyone in your group going for at least three days, preferably five. If you won't eat it, then it won't help keep you going, so be sure to pack food your family will actually eat.

Many people make the mistake of not packing enough

calories in their emergency kits. Things like jerky and granola bars are good choices, but too many salty foods will make you thirsty and cause you to go through your supply of water more quickly. Thrive Life and Mountain House sell instant just-add-hot-water meals that provide more nourishment. Other good choices include:

- Trail mix
- Shelled sunflower seeds
- Small cans of food, such as fruit, ravioli, and tuna
- High calorie energy bars – Handle these with care. High energy may be the last thing your kids need, and if they contain chocolate, they can be messy!
- Hard candies – Offer a prize for whoever can make their Lifesaver last the longest!
- Packets for flavoring water
- Oral rehydration powder – Add to water to speed recovery from dehydration. Pedialyte and RecoverORS are good brands.
- Can opener – Include this even if all your cans have a pop-top because those rings can break.
- Utensils: one fork, spoon and knife per person.

You'll find more handy food options in the Evacuation Supplies Checklist in the Appendix of this book.

Other standard items for an emergency kit include:

- A change of clothing, including extra socks – Bonus points if they are wool.
- A portable radio – There are hand-crank and solar powered versions as well as USB powered.
- A washcloth or compact travel towel – You should always know where your towel is! This is one item with multiple purposes.
- A first aid kit

EMERGENCY EVACUATIONS

- Toiletries and hygiene supplies
- Prescription medication for those with specific medical requirements – Don't forget the EpiPen and/or Benadryl for allergic reactions.
- Waterproof matches or lighter
- Current pictures of family members – These will become important if you are separated and need assistance locating them. For kids, put pictures of you on their tablet or phone in case they wander off and need help finding you.
- Smartphone/tablet chargers – Charger cord and a cube or a crank/solar charger.
- Emergency kits for infants and toddlers – Be sure to include sufficient diapers for at least three days. Keep in mind that even children who are potty-trained may regress during times of emotional stress and it may be hard to find a place for a pit stop during an evacuation, so it might be good to pack a pull-up or two, just in case.
- A pack of cloth diapers and diaper pins – Even if you don't have a child in diapers, they are still an absorbent fabric you can use to wipe up spills, as a sling, as a face mask, etc. (We have thirteen year old cloth diapers that never touched a babies behind, but have done massive amounts of dusting in our house.)
- A flashlight
- Extra batteries for each battery-powered item in your kit – Be sure to rotate and test these!
- Small items to stave off boredom – A book, deck of cards, or small pad of paper with a pen (check the ink periodically) or pencil with a pencil sharpener.
- Books/e-books – Pack or download a good book for

a family read-aloud. Even younger kids enjoy long chapter books when mom or dad is reading to them. Pack or download the Bible or other religious book.
- Emergency Mylar or wool blankets
- Important documents – Create a mini Grab-n-Go binder (discussed in the next section) with copies of only your most vital documents, such as birth certificates, passports, insurance information, etc. It's not a bad idea to store back-ups of these "in the cloud," on a small USB you hand-carry, or at the home of an out-of-state relative.
- Pocket knife or multi-tool with a good blade

No matter what you pack, the kit should be light enough for the intended user to carry it unassisted. That means your kids, spouse, parents, and anyone else with a bag should be able to carry their own bag, unaided and without being injured by excessive weight or a bad fit, for as long as they need to.

When our kids were ages 7 and 9, I packed a cross-shoulder bag for each of them, equipped with a water bottle, Band-Aids, light sticks, and a few other supplies. The bags were inexpensive, I found them on eBay, but they were exactly the right size. It was a relief to not have to carry those extra items *and* it was enormously helpful that they could access what they needed, when they needed it, without asking Mom for help.

The very littlest members won't be able to carry their own full bag, of course, but even toddlers can carry a drink, a snack, and a toy. Have a separate, small kit, indeed, for the little ones, but it should be small enough to be attached to a larger backpack carried by mom or dad.

Practice walking with your kit on your back or slung across

your shoulder for longer and longer distances. A fairly new fitness trend is to carry a weighted backpack on runs in order to increase endurance, so you will only appear to be highly dedicated to physical fitness – just in case you're worried about looking weird!

One final step to take is deciding where to store your kit(s). They should be kept in an easily accessible, though out-of-the-way, location. Everyone in your family should know exactly where they are, and be able to grab them and leave quickly. Don't hide your emergency kits under tennis rackets, behind the Christmas tree deep in the basement, or in an obscure, blocked corner of the garage. At the same time, the middle of the living room is not an appropriate place, either. Many families keep their kits in a closet by the front or back door. In homes without an extra closet, a bottom cupboard in the kitchen or a bathroom near the back door is a good designated spot.

It's not a bad idea to go ahead and pack the emergency kits in your vehicle. The advantage to that, of course, is that it frees you to grab other last minute items as you race for the door. The downside is that the kit contents can become spoiled, rancid, or leak since they will be both out of sight and out of mind. I recommend marking your calendar every six months to check your emergency kit. The spring and fall equinox are easily-remembered dates for this. Replace old food, medicine, and water containers; check to make sure spare shoes and clothes still fit; and refresh the contents if necessary.

Grab-n-Go Binder (vital documents)

Spend a few hours to create a Grab-n-Go binder that contains all your most important documents. It can bring you much peace of mind before, during, and after an evacuation.

When that moment arrives to pack the dogs, the cats, the kids, and the emergency kits, this binder will be waiting and ready to go. From passports to adoption papers to vaccine and other health records, these all need to be in a safe place, organized and together.

If a binder isn't your style, or you just have way too many documents, create a file system in a portable file safe. I use and like the SentrySafe Large File Safe for my documents and family papers.

To make your own Grab-n-Go Binder, you'll need:

- A 2" or larger 3-ring binder
- Plastic page protectors
- Binder dividers
- Your collection of vital documents
- Plastic pockets for holding DVDs and thumb drives

Those documents might include:

Financial documents

- Copies of the fronts and backs of debit and credit cards
- Copies of property deeds and car titles
- Names, addresses, and phone numbers of all banks and credit unions, <u>and</u> passwords to all financial websites, including PayPal
- Other important documents related to employment and/or a family business
- Copies of insurance policies:
  - Life
  - Health
  - Auto

EMERGENCY EVACUATIONS

- Homeowners
- Renters
- Copy of vehicle registrations and maintenance records
- Name, address, and phone number for anyone who sends you a bill, the type of bill, and due dates
- Copies of savings bonds, stocks, and bonds
- Copies of statements from investment firms
- Last year's tax returns

Personal documents — These can be organized by dividers, one section per family member.

- A list of names, addresses, phone numbers, and email addresses of relatives and close friends
- Pet vaccine records
- Copies of:
    - Marriage license
    - Birth certificate
    - Driver's licenses
    - Concealed carry permits
    - Passports
    - Social Security cards
    - Recent photos of each family member and each pet
    - Military documents
    - Diplomas and transcripts
    - Resumes
    - Immunization records
- Fingerprints of each family member

Household documents

- Color photos of the exterior of your house and each room in the house

- Photos of anything of particular value
- Appraisals of valuable objects, such as art, jewelry, and collectibles
- A list of firearm serial numbers
- Receipts for furniture, appliances, electronics, fitness equipment, and other larger, high ticket items
- Extended warranty documentation for appliances and other products
- Copy of rent or lease agreement

Legal documents

- Child custody and/or adoption documentation
- Divorce decrees
- Last Will and Testament
- Copies of living trust or family trust
- DNR (Do Not Resuscitate) documentation
- Copies of both past and current, binding contracts
- Names, addresses, and phone numbers of attorneys

Medical documents

- Copy of health insurance cards
- A list of blood types for each family member
- Names, addresses, and phone numbers of all doctors
- Medical histories of each family member
- A list of current prescription drugs, dosages, and pharmacy contact information
- Copies of medical records and test results for anyone in the family with significant health issues

Along with these paper documents, you might want to include a thumb drive that has most or all of this information digitized and stored. A CD containing a video of your home, interior rooms and its exterior, and shots of your vehicles and any valuables can easily be slipped into a plastic pocket and included in the binder.

Clearly label the binder and store it in an accessible, easy to remember location. Because it contains personal information, it would be invaluable to a thief, so storage in a safe or other very secure location is recommended. Some smart Survival Moms store items like this in bins labeled "Old toys" or "Miscellaneous".

Where should you keep the originals of these documents? If a document can easily be replaced, such as a car insurance policy (simply call your agent or insurance company and ask for a new copy), then keep the original in your binder. Otherwise, store copies only and keep originals in a safe or a safe deposit box.

Does it have to be a backpack?

One question I'm often asked is, "What's the best type of bag for my emergency kit? Does it have to be a backpack?"

Well, it may surprise you, but in some cases, the best bag isn't a bag at all but some other, more versatile container! One mom who has experienced her fair share of hurricane evacuations strongly suggests using a hamper or laundry basket for toting along clothing and other supplies. Eventually, you'll end up with dirty laundry, and it has to go somewhere! A laundry basket is much handier for a trip to the laundromat than a suitcase or backpack.

Most evacuations, by far, will involve some sort of motorized vehicle, and that's good news for you! Instead of planning on relying on only what you can carry, you can utilize various versatile containers that can double as a wash basin or even as an emergency toilet. Here are a few suggestions:

- A metal bucket with lid can hold hot ashes and be used to carry water, firewood, and a whole lot more. Overturned, it makes a sturdy seat.
- Milk crates are made of very sturdy plastic and can be stacked. If you have several of them, you can stack them on their sides to create a handy, temporary shelving system.
- 5-Gallon buckets with lids can hold just about anything and everything you may want to transport. Buy a snap-on toilet seat and some plastic liners, and you have a handy, emergency toilet.
- Rolling suitcases on wheels won't do well over rough terrain, but on sidewalks and paved roads, they're great. It's a big advantage that young children can pull them along without much difficulty, leaving you with one less thing to haul.
- Plastic bins with lids can double as bathtubs for babies and toddlers as well as a wash basin for dirty dishes.

I once heard a story about an elderly lady who was the very last to arrive at the community shelter during a city-wide emergency drill because her 72-hour kit was packed in a giant rolling trash can. While her kit contained a great many useful items, it was so heavy that she needed help from two or three young men to move it. Such a kit would be okay for a vehicle evacuation, but on foot? Not so much.

If you do go for a backpack, try it on for size before making the purchase. You can skimp on less expensive toilet paper, watch for sales on the LifeStraw, but when it comes to your backpack, buy top quality, and be picky about fit.

EMERGENCY EVACUATIONS

The best backpack for long-term walking will have:

- Comfortable, padded shoulder straps
- A hip belt that easily rests over your hip bones
- Load lifters -- This is the set of straps that are located right at shoulder level and help to pull the weight of the load off your shoulders so it's more evenly distributed.
- Sternum straps connect across your chest and help keep the shoulder straps fitting snugly.

My favorite backpack is a neutral color, has all the features listed above plus many compartments, pockets, and padding on the back side. In a crowd, I want to blend in and not stand out like Little Miss Prepper!

Special kits for special family members

An emergency kit for baby

Racing out the door just in time to avoid an encounter with a house fire, flood waters, or a tornado is exactly the right thing to do, but without the basic care items for an infant, you'll soon find yourself in need of a diaper or two, at least! Not having a pacifier or some other supply to keep baby happy will only add to an already high-stress situation.

Preparing an emergency kit for a baby can get a little expensive, since you'll be needing duplicates of just about every baby care supply you use. Watch for coupons in the newspaper and, especially, in parenting magazines. Match those with store sales, and you can save a bundle.

A well-packed and organized diaper bag will probably do just fine if that's all you have prepared, but you might consider having a small, secondary bag as well. That second bag will contain items not kept in the daily-duty diaper bag but will be needed if you have to be away from home for several days. This second kit can be stored with other emergency kits and supplies.

Because babies grow so quickly and their needs change as they mature, make a note on your calendar to review the contents of this particular bag every 3 months, rather than every 6 months.

A basic kit for baby should include:

- A pack of disposable diapers – Even if you use cloth only, you never know where, exactly, your evacuation will take you, nor how long you'll be away from home and the convenience of a washing machine and dryer. Disposables can fill the gap in the meantime. Be sure to rotate these out and replace with a larger size as your baby grows.
- Baby wipes – If your baby has extra sensitive skin and is used to only one brand of wipes, be sure those are what you pack!
- Hand sanitizer or sanitizer wipes
- A few small, plastic trash bags – You'll be glad to have these for containing dirty diapers, wipes, and other trash. A wet bag is a good choice, too.
- 4-6 clothing changes – You can bet that at the worst possible moment, your smiling baby will present you with a diaper blowout or vomit eruption. It will be a relief to have plenty of extra clean clothes on hand! The clothing should have crotch snaps to make it easier to switch from one outfit to another. Again, rotate these as baby grows into bigger sizes.
- Additional clothing, depending on the season – A hat for hot summer weather, cozy socks/slippers

EMERGENCY EVACUATIONS

and a cuddly jacket for winter time are all small items but they make a big difference in comfort and safety.
- 2-3 warm baby blankets – These are multi-purpose items and will probably come in handy for other uses.
- 2-3 burp cloths or cloth diaper
- A pacifier and a back-up pacifier, if your baby needs one
- 7 days' worth of formula and bottles -- If you nurse, disposable breast pads in case of leakage and a spare cover for baby.
- 3-4 days' worth of baby food and a couple of spoons
- Sippy cups
- Purified water for formula and drinking
- A small first aid kit just for baby's needs:
  - Teething gel
  - Nasal aspirator
  - Saline drops
  - Baby thermometer
  - Vaseline
  - Baby safe bug repellent
  - Baby safe sunblock
  - Liquid baby vitamins
  - Baby medicine dropper
  - Gas relief drops
  - Antibiotic cream
- Small bottles of these, if you normally use them:
  - Baby oil
  - Baby lotion
  - Diaper cream
  - Baby powder or cornstarch
  - Baby shampoo

- Baby wash
- 1 or 2 plastic bibs for easy cleaning
- 1 or 2 toys that baby enjoys
- 1 or 2 favorite board book
- An ID bracelet, ID tag for shoes — Anything that your baby can wear that will identify him or her as yours if you get separated

Looks like baby's emergency kit may end up weighing as much as baby!

In addition to these supplies, give some thought to where baby will sleep. A portable crib/playpen is an easy solution. If baby is a little older, a product called My Cot Portable Bed is lightweight and will keep little ones off the ground on a clean, safe sleeping surface.

One final thing to have on hand is one or two baby carriers. I carried both my babies in various slings and wraps and loved the freedom it gave me (both hands were free), and my baby was always with me, comforted by mom's presence.

Visit second hand baby stores to find bargains on baby carriers, portable cribs, small playpens, and other gear you consider necessary for your baby's comfort and your own sanity in an evacuation scenario.

Pet kits

Don't forget about your pets! Each pet should have an emergency kit as well. A sample emergency kit for a dog would include:

- Food – Dry kibble in labeled zip-top bags or cans. Check the expiration date and don't forget a can opener. Canned food has the advantage of containing water, thus requiring less water for drinking.

A few companies make pet energy bars, believe it or not! These aren't nutritionally balanced for long-term feeding but for the short-term they provide calories and nutrients.

- Water – Plan on packing 1 ounce of water per day for every pound your pet weighs.
- Important papers
- Description of the animal (name, species, breed, color, sex, age, distinguishing features)
- Proof of vaccinations – Shelters typically require vaccinations, and immunizations will keep your pet safe from contagious diseases. It's not a bad idea to store back-ups of these "in the cloud" or on a small USB you hand-carry.
- Registration and licensing papers
- List of shelters, boarding facilities, equestrian centers, stables, and pet-friendly hotels within a 50-mile radius of your destination.
- Current photos of the pet – Ideally, include photos taken from both sides. Also include photos that show you and your pet together, to help establish ownership.
- Bedding, towels, blankets
- Bowls for food and water
- Cage, carrier, or kennel for each pet -- Collapsible kennels might be easier to store, or you can use the carrier to hold the pet's 72-hour kit until you need it.
- Trash bags, paper towels
- Can opener, if using canned dog food
- Muzzle – Even gentle pets can become aggressive if

they are stressed or in pain. Soft cloth muzzles are available at pet stores.
- Brush for longer-haired pets
- Leash, extra collar, harness, etc.
- Disposable litter boxes and litter
- A bottle of Kids N Pets Stain and Odor Remover or Nature's Miracle will go a long way to make life a little more bearable in the case of an accident.
- First aid kit with dog-specific items, such as a claw clipper and flea/tick medication.

If your pets aren't used to traveling in a vehicle and, especially, confined to a crate, the time for that training is now. The more accustomed they are to entering a crate and traveling, the easier it will be when, or if, an evacuation ever happens.

In my home, I've designated my daughter as the one responsible for the pets in the early minutes of an evacuation. We've decided that the pets should be contained as quickly as possible to allow us to take care of all the details leading up to driving away. Since she is the one they trust most, she's the logical person to take on this responsibility. Who in your family is most likely to have success containing and loading up the animals? Make that designation part of your evacuation plans.

Grandma's and Grandpa's emergency kits

Another specialized emergency kit is for elderly loved ones. Their needs will be different from yours and younger members of the family. Here are a few considerations as you prepare their kit.
- What medications are they taking? Is it possible to get an extra 30-day supply, just in case getting to a

EMERGENCY EVACUATIONS

pharmacy isn't possible? Ask the doctor for a "vacation" prescription. If a medication needs to be kept refrigerated, that should be noted on a Last Minute List.
- Following an evacuation, a visit may have to be made to a doctor or the hospital. Make a list of each medication, dosage, the name of the doctor who prescribed it, and contact information for the pharmacy. Keep this document with your own emergency kit if you'll be the one in charge of transporting this family member and give a copy to Grandma, in case you get separated from each other.
- Another list to create is one with the names and contact information for all doctors involved in the care of Grandma or Grandpa. Again, keep this list with your own emergency supplies and give a copy to grandparents, in case you end up either separated or not evacuating together. Make sure the names, specialties, and phone numbers for their doctors are in their cell phone, even if they can't use it someone can help them.
- Is there medical equipment that will need to be included in the evacuation? If so, know how to pack up the equipment and have a plan for loading it into your vehicle.
- If Grandma is healthy and independent, give her the gift of a well-stocked emergency kit. Include copies of her vital documents.
- Have a plan for including Grandpa's pet in your evacuation.
- Spend some time with Grandma collecting the most important family heirlooms, photos, and mementos, things that would be devastating to her and the

family if lost. If possible, pack those items together and place them with the emergency kits that are at the ready.

Include your elderly loved ones in your evacuation plans, including any rehearsals that you have planned.

Packing water

The basic rule of thumb when it comes to water is to keep on hand one gallon of water per person per day, unless you live in a hot, desert climate. In that case, I strongly recommend storing 2 gallons per person, per day.

Water weighs 8 pounds per gallon, which makes it difficult to transport when you're traveling by foot. If you think your evacuation may very well include hiking to safety, a portable water filter (or two or three, if they are small) might be a better option. You can use it when you encounter streams, rivers, lakes, and other water sources.

Everyone in your group should have their own water bottle stored in their individual kit. If there's a baby in the house, store purified water for mixing with baby formula, and mom, make sure you stay hydrated, especially if you're nursing!

At least one emergency kit should contain a portable water filter. I have used and recommend the Life Straw, the Sawyer Mini Water Filter, and SteriPEN water purifiers. The latter use ultraviolet light to purify water.

I also recommend keeping a small bottle of unscented bleach in one or more kits, along with an eye dropper. It only takes 8 drops of bleach to purify a gallon of water. If the water is cloudy, use 16 drops. Hopefully your evacuation route will follow regular streets and highways where additional supplies will be available but having one or two methods for purifying water is a small addition to a pack but brings a lot of peace of mind.

If you are traveling by car, consider investing in a few Waterbricks. These contain 3.5 gallons of water each and only weigh about thirty pounds when full. The modular design means you can easily stack them in your vehicle.

Comfort items for stressful times

The purpose of an emergency kit is to help sustain you and your loved ones in an emergency. If your children have items used for comfort, such as a favorite blanket, stuffed animal, or doll, those are nearly as important as any other must-have in your kit. It may seem trivial, but these items can greatly ease a child's stress in a crisis and will make your job as a parent much easier. Conversely, a child without their favorite comfort object will be much more difficult to soothe and this will, in turn, increase the stress on you, the parent and on everyone else in the group.

This is even truer for many special needs kids whose comfort item(s) helps maintain their emotional and psychological balance.

Comfort items are more difficult to keep track of because children may leave them anywhere in the house. In an urgent evacuation, you will not have time to search through all the laundry to find your child's blankie. When push comes to shove, favorite toys will have to be left behind – your lives are certainly worth more than a stuffed animal – but be aware that it will come at a cost.

Beth, a young Survival Mom, tells the story of one of the most traumatic experiences in her life that occurred when her family had to run to catch a train. After the family was boarded and the train door closed behind them, her four-year-old had the biggest ever emotional meltdown because he had dropped his favorite toy on the train platform. Fortunately, they were able to retrieve it, but to this day, that experience is unforgettable!

Elderly parents may have some comfort items as well, particularly mementos of a lost loved one they cannot bear to be without or lose. If you can help it at all, bring those items with you. Have them pre-packed if they aren't currently being used or displayed.

Case Study: Evacuating a special needs loved one

Lorraine is a good friend of mine and has told me a bit about her family's evacuation plans. They have given this a lot of thought, more than most people, because her younger sister, Kay, is an adult with Down syndrome. They know that Kay will have a very difficult time handling the intense stress that can be a part of an evacuation.

At 47 years old, Kay is a moderate functioning, independent minded woman. She lives in a small, rural town with her parents. They've identified hurricane force storms and wildfires as their most likely foes and have planned accordingly.

Kay has been given a set of 4 specific instructions, along with the family's code words, "Bug out!" She may not know exactly why they're leaving or specifically where they're going but she does know to do the following:

1. Get your emergency kit.
2. Gather your security items.
3. Take those out to the car.

EMERGENCY EVACUATIONS

> 4. Return to the house to help Dad get into car and then stay there with him.

Kay's dad has mobility issues and will need extra help. This final task keeps her attention focused while Mom loads the car with everything else, secures the house, and then gets ready to drive away.

As Lorraine explained this plan to me, she emphasized the need to carefully consider the needs, abilities, and temperament of the special needs person. In the case of her sister, there are <u>many</u> security, or comfort, items she's attached to, but her parents have made it clear that she probably won't be able to bring all of them. "She'd bring her whole bedroom if she could!" Lorraine joked. Kay tends toward obsessive compulsive disorder (OCD), which is something the family takes into consideration.

Several years ago I received an email from the worried mom of a young man who was significantly autistic. Like Kay, he was OCD but was the size of a grown man and impossible for his mom to physically handle when he became upset.

She said, "Lisa, I'm scared to death about a possible evacuation because there's no way I can physically get him into my vehicle. When he becomes emotional, it's impossible to do anything with him and he'll actually fight against me."

A situation like this poses a moral dilemma for parents and other loved ones, and there are no easy answers. Is it right to abandon the one they love and hope he or she survives so that the rest of the family can reach safety? Should one parent stay with the special needs family member while everyone else leaves?

The recommendation I gave to this worried mom is a decision that is ultimately between parent and the family physician. Consult with a doctor who knows your loved one well about a sedative that is as risk free as possible, yet effective, and keep several doses on hand. This is one of those "In case of emergency, break glass," solutions -- something used rarely and only in the most extreme scenarios, a life or death situation.

As well, pay close attention to anything and everything that triggers extreme emotional reactions. In the case of Kay, her family has taught her simple, structured steps in a non-threatening, unemotional setting and they have rehearsed them with her. They know that her security items hold high value with her, so they have included those items as part of her evacuation routine.

What can you absolutely, positively not leave behind?

A few years ago I found myself sitting in our living room with nothing to do. I gazed at bookshelves filled with books and souvenirs from our family's travels, and the thought occurred to me, "If the house caught on fire, what would I grab first?" I spent some time reviewing each shelf, our stack of DVDs, and the contents of a few drawers and realized that there wasn't anything in that room worth saving!

Over the next few days and weeks, I went through the same thought process in every other room, including our bathrooms! I ended up with a fairly short list of things that I couldn't bear to lose. Eventually, most of those items made their way into a small safe, while others are still scattered around the house for various reasons.

EMERGENCY EVACUATIONS

A quick five-minute room scan is a great way to select your most important belongings well ahead of an urgent, panic-filled evacuation when decisions will be difficult, if not impossible, to make. Once you've determined which items you absolutely, positively cannot leave behind, then you can make plans for securing them. Those plans might include storing them in a safe or safe deposit box, adding them to your Last Minute Packing List, or, if they're small enough, keeping them with your evacuation kits and supplies.

The important thing is to first identify them.

Spend just a few minutes scanning each room and going through cupboards, shelves, and cabinets. This will take less time than you think and you, like me, will almost certainly be shocked at how few things fall into this top priority category.

Everything you identify will probably fall into one of these three categories:

1. Vital documents

2. Items of value

- Cash
- Jewelry
- Heirlooms
- Precious metals
- Firearms
- Antiques
- Collections
- Art

3. Items of sentimental value

- Photos and photo albums – Don't forget framed

photos on the wall. Those can be grabbed at the last minute and stashed in a plastic bin, cardboard box, or even a heavy duty plastic trash bag.

- Memory box contents
- Handmade treasures
- Particularly treasured gifts
- Sentimental collections, not of any particular monetary value
- Others?

Ideally, find a safe place in which to store all these items and keep them near an exit point in your home. Vital documents can be stored together in a Grab-n-Go binder as well as scanned and stored electronically on a thumb drive or the Cloud via Dropbox or Google Drive.

If smaller items are already occupying space in a cupboard or are otherwise out of sight, you may as well store them together in a box or bin. Keep that box with your emergency kits so it will be ready to grab and go, whether your evacuation is urgent or planned.

There will be items that need to be itemized on your Last Minute Packing List, such as cash, firearms, and memorabilia. Indicate on the list where each thing will be stored for the evacuation and the person in charge of securing it.

The last minute packing list

No matter how well-prepared you may be, there will be items that simply cannot be packed until the very last minute. In the flurry of getting ready to leave the house, these vital items could be left behind if you don't have a list posted in a handy place.

EMERGENCY EVACUATIONS

In addition to creating and posting the Last Minute List, you should include grabbing these items at the very last minute and assign individuals responsible for each one. Here are a few things that might be on your own Last Minute List:

1. Cash — In many instances, ATM machines and banks won't be readily available. In many emergencies, with many people making withdrawals, ATM machines run out of cash quickly. Always have a few hundred dollars in small bills, $20 and smaller, in a handy location in the house. This gives you an advantage when purchasing gasoline, food, or paying for a hotel.

   One Survival Mom told me about purposely withdrawing $500 per day in the days leading up to a hurricane evacuation. She said, "When we returned, the banks and ATM machines in our town weren't operating yet. That cash gave us the means to purchase what we needed from stores and businesses that managed to reopen."

2. Medications — Any prescription or over-the-counter medications that cannot be pre-packed in your emergency kits should be added to your Last Minute Packing List.

3. Medical equipment — This includes wheelchairs, walkers, CPAP machines, a nebulizer, or a diabetic meter with test strips.

4. Equipment or supplies required by a special needs family member

5. Firearms and extra magazines and ammunition — Decide now what you will grab at the last minute. If you plan on taking a specific handgun with you, it's a

good idea to have it already packed in your bag, along with an extra couple of magazines and ammo.

Make sure that all other firearms are in a heavy-duty gun safe in order to keep them safe from theft, fire, and flood while you're gone. The safe should be bolted to the floor.

6. Appropriate clothing for current and forecasted weather conditions – In spite of pre-packing your emergency kits, you don't know exactly what the weather will be like when the evacuation occurs or what to expect at your final destination. Such items could include rain gear, heavy duty coats, or even bathing suits.

7. Heirlooms and valuables – Ideally, these should already be in a fire-proof safe, if possible. Otherwise, know their locations around the house so they can be grabbed quickly. If they aren't on display, then collect the valuables that are most important to you and store them in a portable, locked safe with your emergency kits. This will be one last thing to worry about grabbing as you leave the house.

8. Photo albums – Plan on grabbing those that have the most sentimental value. Again, keep them in a bin or other container with your evacuation supplies.

9. Small safes or strong-boxes – These likely contain important documents and, possibly, items of value. They should be in a location that is easily accessible and not so heavy that they can't be carried.

Keep in mind that good quality safes are designed to withstand fire and water damage. You purchased them and filled them with important belongings for just such

EMERGENCY EVACUATIONS

a time as this! Don't risk your life trying to lug a heavy safe out of your home when seconds count. Leave it behind and trust that it will do its job.

10. Precious metals – Don't leave these behind for burglars or Mother Nature's fury. They can be very heavy so you might want to either store them in multiple smaller containers or assign the task of packing them to the strongest person in the family.

    In general, I don't recommend storing all your precious metals together in one location.

11. Vital electronics – Anything regularly used to keep personal and financial records should be included on your Last Minute List. If it's a laptop, be sure to grab the charger. If time is of the essence and you only have a desktop computer, assign someone to unplug the CPU and pack it up.

12. All vital documents, including insurance policies, health records, passports, birth and marriage certificates – Create a Grab-n-Go binder in order to have all these in one location. You'll find instructions for making your own binder on page 57.

13. Perishable foods – A cooler filled with fruit and other fresh, ready-to-eat foods will help you stay on your route longer and avoid stopping at fast food joints or convenience stores. You'll get to your final destination more quickly. You also won't have to worry that rotting produce will damage your fridge.

14. Comfort items for family members – These could include favorite blankets, stuffed animals, and/or pillows. You may be tempted to leave these behind, but do so at your own peril!

15. Family pets and their supplies – In all the hustle and bustle of the evacuation, please don't leave behind your pets to fend for themselves.

16. Camping supplies, just in case – You may be in an urgent evacuation mode with no real destination in mind, other than the hope of reaching a hotel by nightfall. With a tent, sleeping bags, and a few other camping basics, you'll be equipped to set up your own temporary shelter. This also comes in handy if you end up at a relative's home and there's not enough sleeping room for your family.

17. School supplies – It would be such a shame for the kids to be displaced from home and school for several days, or longer, and not be able to continue their school work! So round up textbooks, assignments, pencils, and other supplies. This step will help a great deal in establishing a sanity-saving routine if your evacuation lasts more than a few days.

Use these suggestions to create your own Last Minute Packing list using the printable checklist found in the Appendix of this book. Post it somewhere near your emergency supplies and include a copy in the front of your Grab-n-Go Binder.

In the chaos of an evacuation, it will be extremely important that each person knows exactly what their responsibility is. Include on the list the name of the person responsible for each last minute packing item and the location(s) for each item. You may not be the one in charge of this evacuation and may not even be at home when it occurs, so make your Last Minute Packing List as easy to follow as possible.

As with everything having to do with emergency

preparedness, you are never "done" putting together your emergency kit and plans. It's not enough to merely obtain these items; prepping is not about the stuff you have, it's a way of life. You have to constantly maintain your kit by rotating out food that is about to expire, ensure that clothing always fits and is appropriate for the weather and season (especially crucial for kits belonging to fast-growing children!), and regularly test the stored batteries for efficacy. There is nothing more depressing than opening up your emergency kit when it's needed, looking forward to something that resembles a decent meal, only to discover that your granola bars expired five years ago and now taste like kindergarten paste, and your flashlight batteries corroded, leaving it useless.

The All-Important Staging Area

One of the most important concepts my husband ever taught me was the importance of having a staging area established for each family vacation.

Our kids quickly learned where the staging area was, typically near the back door, and it became second nature to tell them, "Go put your stuff in the staging area." When it came time to leave, everything we needed to bring was on that one specific area.

I highly recommend that you begin this practice, too, whether it's for an evacuation, vacation, or just getting ready to head out to baseball practice. Determine where a good area would be for suitcases, pillows, an ice chest, and all your other supplies, and begin utilizing that space as your family's official "Staging Area." The kids will catch on in no time.

Once everything is in its place, you can then pull out your

evacuation checklists and mark off each item. It will be easy to identify anything, or anyone, who might be missing.

> **TIP**: As part of your packing and planning, give some thought to establishing a communications hub. This will be a person living some distance from you with whom you will check in at regular intervals. Provide them with a copy of your route, including pre-planned detours, if they become necessary, and phone numbers for each of your stopping points and final destination.
>
> They should also have your email addresses and the cell phone numbers for each person in your group.
>
> This person, in turn, can pass along information and messages to you from other family members or friends as well as up to date news about the weather, disaster, and other relevant events.

Think outside the box when it comes to evacuation destinations

Your kits are ready, the pets and kids are bundled up and you've remembered to grab their favorite play toys and diversions, but now the big question remains, where do you go?

Remember that if your end destination is more than a day's travel away, you'll need places to spend the night along your planned route.

If you're like the majority of Americans, you don't own a second home and don't have friends who live on rural ranches or farms. Those are all considered to be "safer" spots for long-term evacuations, but what other options are there? Obviously, staying with grandparents, siblings, or other relatives and close friends are locations that will be at the top of your list. But if those destinations aren't viable for some reason, here are a few more to consider:

Campgrounds

Camping is one of the very best activities you and your family can experience to help prepare you for survival scenarios. You're providing your own shelter, heat (if needed), using off-grid methods for cooking and sanitation, and banding together to not only survive the wilderness but have a fun time as well. If you own basic camping gear and have at least some skills for selecting a good campsite, pitching a tent, safely starting and building a fire, cooking food, and procuring water, then evacuating to a campground is a good choice.

If campgrounds are full, then get out your map and head for a state or national park that allows primitive, or dispersed, camping. This is camping anywhere other than a designated campground and you won't have access to any facilities. Find out which parks allow that and what their rules are.

Urban camping

This option is a possibility for both tent camping and RV/trailer camping. Some businesses, such as Wal-Mart, allow overnight RV camping in their parking lots. If you're very subtle about it, you can park for a night or two in an apartment complex parking lot or at 24-hour grocery stores if you have no other options. You'll need to have all your supplies very well organized, with the items you'll need most easily accessible. During the day, you can go to a local park for some fresh air, a picnic, and to let the kids play. For a family, this isn't an easy option unless you have an RV.

Camping on friends' property

You may not have friends with spacious homes or homesteads, but just about everybody has a friend who would allow them to "urban camp" in their backyard or driveway. They may not have sleeping space for you, but would gladly allow you to use their bathroom and laundry facilities, and share meals.

Mobile home park

If you own an RV, you may be able to park it, temporarily, at a mobile home park. Call ahead to check their regulations since many are set by the city or state.

Hotels

These can be pricey and if ATM machines in the area are down, you'll have to be prepared with enough cash to cover the expense. However, there's virtually no preparation involved, other than calling ahead to get a reservation. If you have pets, you can find pet-friendly hotels at BringFido.com. Hotels are far less accommodating when it comes to cats, but cat-friendly hotels do exist.

Timeshares

If you're like millions of timeshare owners, you probably have extra weeks banked. These resorts are an excellent destination because timeshare units often include laundry facilities and full kitchens. Many also have scheduled activities, which will help a great deal for keeping the kids occupied.

Call your timeshare company directly, explain your situation, and ask for their help. Be flexible with your destinations, don't insist on a 5-star deluxe resort — but if one is available, by all means, grab it!

Airbnb

Started in 2008, Airbnb is a fairly new travel concept. Homeowners with extra space for visitors open their homes to travelers on a short term basis. You may end up sleeping on the floor on futons or get a spacious room, or more, all to yourself. Check out the website, read the terms, and look for locations near your evacuation routes. And, as with any other type of accommodation, take care and stay situationally aware.

Youth hostels

Back in the day, I stayed in hostels all over Europe and noticed plenty of families with kids of all ages as well as adults of all ages who were also taking advantage of this very low-cost option. Most hostels are definitely no-frills but will cost about $15-40 or so per night, which is a huge savings over any hotel or motel. There aren't nearly as many hostels in the U.S. as there are in Europe, but you might get lucky and find ones along your evacuation route. Visit the Hostelling International (hiusa.org) and Hostels.com websites to learn more.

Stay with friends of friends

When my husband moved to Texas, ahead of our family, he was welcomed into the home of a homeschooling family we had never met. The arrangement came about from a simple request on the homeschooling group's forum. It was a blessing for us, and we would do the same for another family in need. If you have connections through a church, homeschool organization, social clubs, and the like, you may be able to find just the right, temporary destination for your family's evacuation. Don't be afraid to ask and let your needs be known.

Non-government shelters

If the thought of checking in to a FEMA shelter gives you

EMERGENCY EVACUATIONS

the willies, then keep your eyes and ears open to temporary shelter facilities at churches, schools, and other public buildings. Organizations such as The Salvation Army often coordinate with local businesses and government to get these set up quickly. In fact, in most cases, these shelters will be up and running long before FEMA officials even complete their lengthy paperwork. That's the nature of bureaucracy.

If you do find yourself heading for a public shelter, here are a few things you should know:

- Be prepared for a nearly complete loss of privacy.
- Bring your own food and water. There may be some available, but having your own will be much better than standing in line.
- Pets will not be allowed but service animals are.
- Adults and older children/teens should take turns keeping an eye on family belongings. Don't assume that anything is theft-proof.
- Keep cash and other valuables stored out of sight in your locked car. If you have to bring anything in that you don't want to be stolen, a small security safe, like a pistol safe, is handy for storing prescription drugs, cash, ID papers, and other small, important items.
- Be sure to bring chargers for your electronics, an extension cord, and a multi-plug outlet.
- Bring bedding, pillows, and towels from home.
- Pack pajamas or something modest for sleeping. You'll likely be in a large room filled with cots and many strangers.

Learn from the homeless

I'm not eager to recommend this, but in some cases, you may be homeless for a while, from just overnight to several days or more. No one said living out of a car, truck, or other vehicle would be easy, but hundreds of thousands of people do it every day. If you are well and truly stuck, these tips passed on to me from a few folks who lived the homeless lifestyle may help:

- Get organized and stay organized! Have a place for everything and make sure everyone in the group knows where to find things and to put everything back in the same place. There's no shorter route to insanity than having to search for every single thing you need, especially if the need is urgent.
- Keep a family toiletry bag handy with a bar of soap, washcloth, toothbrushes, toothpaste, deodorant, and any other items needed for freshening up. You can find showers at truck stops and KOA campgrounds, usually for a small fee. If you belong to the YMCA, you can use their facilities anywhere in the U.S.
- Pack lightweight, thin towels. They'll dry faster.
- Have a small, plastic basin handy for washing dishes, hand-washing small batches of laundry, and bathing. A dishpan or 5 gallon bucket will work just fine for these purposes.
- If you have freeze-dried meals, this is where that investment may really pay off. They're very lightweight and can be prepared in minutes. An immersion heater can heat up the water quickly and those are available with the standard electrical plug and one that plugs into your car's power socket.
- Always use window shades in your vehicle for

privacy.
- If possible, attach a tarp to your vehicle or nearby trees for another area of shelter.
- Do not use candles inside your vehicle. Rely on flashlights, headlamps, and other sources of light.
- Libraries have computers and internet access, which you'll need to contact your insurance agent, employer, friends, and family.

Staying sane under (very) trying circumstances!

Most survival guides never touch on one of the most important aspects of survival: staying sane. A family of five, trapped in a minivan that is both their transportation and their lodging is soon going to be walking a shaky line between sanity and glassy-eyed crazy.

Packing the emergency kits, gathering together important documents, deciding where to go, and mapping out safe routes are the easy part of an evacuation. Actually hitting the road, unsure what lies ahead of you or for how long you'll be gone, breeds fear, uncertainty, and conflict. Lots and lots of conflict.

Much of this can be avoided.

Sanity supplies

First, on my master Evacuation Supplies Checklist, you'll notice that I've included a special category: Sanity. Take that category just as seriously as Sanitation and Sustenance. Your emergency supplies and kits should be equipped with items that will help keep each family member occupied and entertained.

Whenever my family goes on a long road trip, and we've covered more than 16,000 miles, I end up reading aloud.

Over those long miles, my kids listened to me read the entire *Percy Jackson* and *The Kane Chronicles* series, both by Rick Riordan. When I was reading *Sign of the Beaver* by Elizabeth George Speare, I couldn't help but notice that my husband was every bit as attentive as the two kids!

Be sure to pack one or two longer chapter books, even if your kids are quite young. When my kids were 4 and 5 years old and just learning to read, they still enjoyed *The Magic Treehouse* book series by Mary Pope Osborne whenever I read them aloud. Hundreds of great books can be stored on a Kindle or other e-reader and will be a great resource for both entertainment and education.

Don't overlook the CD player! Bring along a good selection of both music CDs and books on CD. If you have a smart phone or tablet, you can also download podcasts to listen to. There are "Ted Talks" on every subject under the sun, and, of course, Survival Mom podcasts!

A portable DVD player is a godsend when it comes to filling long hours on the road or in a hotel. If two kids will be sharing one DVD player, you might want to get a headphone splitter so they can both listen and you don't have to.

Establish a routine

One of the most important pieces you can put into place during this time of chaos and unfamiliar surroundings is a routine. I can't stress enough the importance of having a planned schedule for time spent in the car as well as a schedule of activities once you arrive at your destination.

That routine should include fun activities, chores that help the new "household" run smoothly, and some education. If you've lived through the long summer months with a

EMERGENCY EVACUATIONS

bevy of bored kids, you know how unbearable those long, unstructured hours can become for everyone in the house.

Your Evacuation Daily Schedule could include:

- Daily chores for each family member
- Established meal times — Schedule meal prep and clean-up.
- Quiet time — Either naps or quiet reading.
- Laundry day
- Organization day — After 2 or 3 days, things may gradually fall apart with clothes and belongings strewn everywhere. Take an hour or two to tidy up — almost as good as spring cleaning.
- Scheduled favorite TV shows, possibly on DVD
- Family meetings — Discuss decisions, issues, conflicts, and let everyone express their thoughts and feelings.
- Outings:
    - Go to a movie
    - Visit a museum or other city attractions
    - Go to the mall
    - Go to a sports event
    - Public swimming pool
    - Dog park, if you have dogs
    - Visit nearby friends and relatives
    - Neighborhood park
    - Library — During the summer there will be special events for kids.
    - Nearby national and state parks
- Read-aloud time
- Separate parent/child outings — My kids love these and look forward to them
- School work – The kids will likely whine, but this is a

great way to fill time as well as ensure they will maintain their skill levels once school resumes.

Be sure to write out each day's schedule and post it, both as a reminder to you and to give everyone in the family something to look forward to the next day. If your displacement goes on for more than a week or two, add a "Surprise" to the calendar to add some excitement, even if it's just a visit to Sonic for slushies or Dunkin' Donuts for hot chocolate.

Final considerations

Keep in mind that in most cases, you only need to evacuate to a safer location — away from the flames and smoke of a wildfire or flooding, etc. Sometimes we think we must evacuate many miles away but that isn't always the case. Your "safer place" might just be to your aunt's house across town.

In some cases, though, you <u>will</u> have a longer journey to safety. If you're evacuating ahead of a hurricane or escaping the damage of a flood or earthquake, make sure your planned destination(s) are far enough away to provide real safety. Rain and wind from a hurricane can travel hundreds of miles inland, for example. (More details for that coming up in the next chapter.)

One final consideration when planning possible destinations is the length of time you can feasibly stay in each place. Some scenarios become so dire that coming back home, except to gather whatever belongings remain, is impossible. In that case, could you stay with your in-laws indefinitely? Do you have the right equipment to continue camping long-term?

Wherever you end up, do your best to stay organized,

EMERGENCY EVACUATIONS

keep the kids occupied, and establish a daily routine. These three actions will go a long way toward preserving your sanity.

LISA BEDFORD

Hitting the road

Multiple, planned routes

One of the most important concepts when it comes to survival is having options. The more, the better. When you plan your evacuation route (where to go and how to get there) having multiple options for both will make the actual process less stressful.

In our neck of the woods, we have a large city about an hour south, lakes and forests to the east and northwest, and miles of suburbs to the west. Depending on the type of emergency we face, any one of those directions might be the best one to take, but if we've only planned one route heading north and a forest fire stands in our way, we'd have to make quick decisions on the fly, and who wants to face that additional challenge under extreme duress?

It's best to have planned several routes, each going in different directions. Ultimately, you may end up at the same destination. You've just taken the safest route to get there, under the circumstances.

Use a very detailed road map to mark each route. I've been using the DeLorme atlas and appreciate its detail. As you seek out multiple evacuation routes, continue to look for possible destinations, such as state parks, campgrounds, or logging roads. A good map or atlas will also include back roads and even hiking trails to help you come up with more options than you'll probably need.

Route considerations

What surrounds you in all directions?

Take a few minutes and consider the terrain and population centers that surround you. Use a detailed map, preferably topographic, to examine the terrain about you in all four directions, north, south, east, and west. Take note of potential obstacles, such as bodies of water, bridges, flood zones, large cities, and heavily traveled routes. It's best to be aware of those things now, before you run into an inescapable traffic jam.

On the map, begin tracing possible evacuation routes that will likely be best, with fewest obstacles. Topographic maps show elevation, so you can avoid dangers such as flood-prone areas and bottlenecks such as canyons.

Where will each route lead you?

For each route that you've established, decide on a concrete destination, even if it's a hotel, timeshare, the home of a relative, or a campsite (bring camping gear). If you'll be taking pets, make sure your destination is pet-friendly. Don't invest time in planning routes only to declare, "We'll figure out where to stay when we get there!" Luck may not be on your side when you need it most.

Additionally, identify stopping points that may come in handy or become necessary. Ideally, your route should contain at least 2 or 3 different stopping points, so you have more flexibility and can adapt your plans according to changing circumstances. These points could simply be highway rest stops.

Include these stopping points even if your end destination is only a few hours away. If, after just 2 or 3 hours into your journey everyone, including the driver, is exhausted, you'll be glad to have those intermittent stopping points pre-planned. If one of them is a campground or a town with a hotel, you're better off stopping for the night and continuing to your destination in the morning. Don't underestimate the toll stress will take on you, mentally, emotionally, and physically, and the amount of rest everyone will need.

Circle these stopping points with a pen or Sharpie, along with the final destination at the end of each route.

Plan appropriate routes for different scenarios

A final consideration is which disasters are most likely in your area. List those and then determine in which direction(s) would be safest for evacuating. Add to that list possible destinations, both for short-term, less than six days, and long-term, a week or more.

Your destination may vary, depending on what type of disaster you are facing, so spend a little time thinking through your options. In a flood scenario, you might be okay making a 20-minute drive to higher ground. For something like a hurricane, however, even going an hour down the coast is not going to cut it; you may have to drive as many as three or four hours further inland.

Be ready for traffic nightmares

Along with determining multiple routes, part of your evacuation planning will need to take traffic and crowd issues into consideration.

EMERGENCY EVACUATIONS

When my family lived in Phoenix, we occasionally headed north to the cool country over holiday weekends. Everyone else seemed to have the same idea and sometimes the traffic backed up for miles. Add an overheated car or two, and you could sit there, in the heat, for an hour or more.

Hurricane Rita in 2005, is another excellent example of a disaster within a disaster. Most of downtown Houston was complete wall-to-wall, bumper-to-bumper traffic. More fatalities occurred as a result of poor evacuation planning than from the hurricane itself!

Be prepared to have some tough competition for gas, food, and hotel rooms if most of your city is also evacuating. Heavy traffic also means you'll be on the road longer than anticipated and using more resources (gas, snacks, time) than you'd normally expect. Keep that in mind.

Gasoline, in particular, may become a huge issue. Why? Most people will stop at the gas station they can see from the highway and these will become overloaded in no time. It's even possible that law enforcement will be called in to keep order and possibly enforce the temporary rationing of gas.

Why endure that hassle when there might be a perfectly good gas station a mere five or six blocks away with virtually no line and lower prices? GasBuddy is a free smartphone app that helps you find nearby gas stations and their current prices per gallon. This could be a life-saver for locating out of the way stations.

If the power is out over a large area, gas station pumps won't be operational since they rely on electricity. Even if you plan to reach a safe destination within an hour or two, it would be wise to bring along 2 or 3 filled 5-gallon gas cans to ensure that you get to where you're going and don't end up sleeping in your car, waiting for AAA. Just idling your car for about 15 minutes uses a quarter of a gallon of gas, so plan accordingly.

> **TIP:** Try to leave either very, very early in the morning or late at night. Most people won't be ready for an evacuation at, say 4 a.m., and, at the other end of the day, a lot of people don't like to drive at night. By getting on the road within either of these time frames, you have a good chance of enjoying empty roads, without traffic jams or stalled vehicles and of having the kids fall asleep in the car.

Practice driving your routes

Drive your planned routes ahead of time and scout for out-of-the-way gas stations, mini-marts, dog parks, playgrounds, and lesser known rest areas. Parks, in general, will be a better place to stop for stretching and a bathroom break. Since they will most likely be off the beaten path, the restrooms won't be as overcrowded and nasty as highway rest areas. In an emergency, this knowledge could pay huge dividends in terms of better availability of goods and shorter lines. Be sure to mark those locations and routes on a map that you keep with your emergency kit.

Most smartphones are equipped with a basic GPS system, but it is good to have a backup GPS system in case cell phone coverage is impacted. Keep paper maps in your car or in your emergency kit that cover the area of the entire evacuation route and areas nearby, in case you hit a detour. Some folks have road maps for each state bordering their own, in case unforeseen circumstances require them to travel further than they planned. Both AAA and Welcome Stations for tourists (especially near the state border) are great areas for free maps.

As you head out of town, other vehicles may be part of your convoy. In that case, each vehicle and driver should be equipped with identical maps with routes, rest stops, safe houses, and final destinations clearly marked. Laminate these marked maps and they'll last forever.

Your getaway vehicle: not just for bank robbers!

We've talked about the basics of emergency evacuations, what you should bring with you, and where to go, but what about actually getting to that safe place? You will not get very far if your vehicle is not kept in good condition. This is easily overlooked in the hustle and bustle of daily life, and that comes from a woman who once let her tires get so bald they were as smooth as a baby's bottom!

Starting now, treat your car to regular maintenance, even if it means making advance appointments for things like oil changes, much as you do hair and dental appointments. By taking your car in for regular oil changes and check-ups, your mechanic will be able to spot potential problems before they start. You will know that you can depend on your car when it really counts, and you will prolong the overall life of your car to boot. You can also learn how to do basic maintenance such as oil changes and checking / fixing your tire pressure at home.

Here's what I mean by prolonging the life of your car. In 2006, a friend received a gift from her mother-in-law: a '94 Chevy station wagon. The car was already so old that her mother-in-law expected that it probably wouldn't last for more than six months. However, my friend and her husband were very nearly desperate for transportation and took the car. Undaunted by its age and condition, they were very diligent about taking it to the mechanic at regular intervals and making minor repairs as needed. That car is still running today, in 2015! It runs very well, continues to be reliable, and nothing leaks. That station wagon is ready to hit the road on any emergency evacuation! That's what regular maintenance and attention can do.

Another small detail overlooked by the majority of drivers is a simple one: fuel. Many of us regularly drive on a tank of gas that is less than half full, but it's good to keep your gas tank at least half full. Urgent evacuations cannot be anticipated. You can't be sure that you *won't* be required to hop in your car and drive as far away as quickly as you can with no time to stop for gas on your way out of town. Make it a point to keep a close eye on your gas gauge and be willing to take just five or six minutes to fill it up when it hits the half-full mark.

The next time your gas meter drifts dangerously close to the left of the big, red 'E,' imagine what it would feel like to be stuck on the side of the road with no gas at that very moment. Whatever and whoever you have with you will be your survival reality until help comes along. That's what emergency preparedness is all about: Being well aware of worst case scenarios. By making just the tiniest change in your habits and filling up the car when the tank is still half full, you will be able to avoid this scenario entirely.

Following some types of emergencies, such as an earthquake or hurricane, fuel may be scarce. When Hurricane Rita hit in 2005, one Survival Mom's father made a special trip to fill up the family cars the night before the storm was expected to make landfall. The gas station wasn't terribly busy at the time, and both cars still had a reasonable amount of gas in them, but he filled them up anyway. He also filled a 5-gallon gas can.

Once Rita passed, power lines were down and shipment of gasoline and other goods was disrupted. Cars were lined up around the block to get gas. By then the problem was twofold: some gas stations in our town ran out of gas completely while others had gas, but no electricity to pump it into the cars. Because this dad took an extra 20 minutes to fill up his cars ahead of time, that family didn't have to worry about fuel until the crisis was resolved.

The same principle can be applied to keeping your electronic devices charged. If you rely on a cell phone, GPS, or other electronics, having them fully charged will give you peace of mind that you will be able to rely upon your devices during those times when they are most needed. Invest in a heavy duty external battery pack and possibly a solar charger for charging those devices when the power is out or an electric outlet isn't accessible.

Equip your vehicle for emergencies

In addition to keeping your gas tank full and electronics charged, keep extra supplies in the trunk of your car to be ready for everyday emergencies as well as a possible evacuation.

Stashing containers of automotive fluids like antifreeze and oil in your vehicle is a good idea. It is also wise to keep emergency blankets or a spare 72-hour kit in your car. In this way, if you had to evacuate while you were already away from home, or if the nature of your urgent evacuation means you didn't make it out of the house with your individual emergency kits, you will still have basic provisions.

Supplies for your Vehicle 72-Hour kit

- Blankets – I keep these rolled up tightly, secured with a zip tie, and stored underneath the back seat.
- Light sources – Headlamps are great and leave your hands free, but cheapie light sticks double as a source of entertainment for bored children. Do have a very bright LED flashlight in your vehicle, always.
- Rain ponchos
- Duct tape
- Hand and foot warmers – These should be rotated out, because they can lose efficacy after their expiration date.
- Rope
- Knife – A pocket knife is better than nothing, but you'll be grateful if you pack something sturdier.
- Battery/solar-powered emergency radio
- Ground cover – I pack two large heavy-duty plastic tablecloths. They're inexpensive and can also be used to cover dirty picnic tables.
- Work gloves – You'll need them if you have to change a tire or clear away branches and rubble.
- Extra batteries for anything battery powered in your kit
- Sturdy umbrella – A hurricane is not the place for a cheap umbrella.
- Waterproof matches
- Whistle
- Water purification tablets
- Small portable water filter

- Mirror for signaling
- Small, sturdy shovel – Get a collapsible shovel if space is tight.
- Two heavy duty black trash bags (not kitchen trash bags)
- Dust face masks, especially if you live in an area prone to wildfires

Evacuation on foot

In the midst of chaos and danger, evacuating in a vehicle is a best case scenario. It allows you to get away quickly, travel farther, and gives you many different options. However, in some cases, you may have to travel on foot, and if you have less than 3 miles or so to reach a safer area, walking might actually be quicker than driving if traffic is heavy.

One urban emergency planner stated, "If evacuation volumes are over 5,000 persons per square mile, walking is more efficient; if volumes are less than 5,000 persons per square mile, driving is more efficient."[1]

Even though evacuation by vehicle is more likely, some thought and planning should be given to getting out on foot. Car break-downs or encountering impassable roads will require that you carry with you what you can and progress on foot.

If your situation is not an urgent one and you have time to choose between evacuating by foot or vehicle, consider these points in your planning.

Carry with you only the most vital supplies

To prepare for a long walk or bicycle ride, if that is your choice, first, be familiar enough with your emergency supplies that you could sort through them in a hurry and pick out only items most vital to your survival. Many of us carry nice-to-have items, such as a small sewing kit, but in an extreme, urgent evacuation that now requires you to travel by foot, you'll have to be picky about what you carry. Even a few small items add to the weight of a bag or pack. Remember, some items, such as tools and entertainment, can be shared amongst your group.

You'll need to keep your hands free

For the purpose of a walking or bicycle evacuation, all kits should be contained in backpacks, a shoulder or messenger bag, or any other type of pack that allows you to keep your arms and hands free. You'll need those to hold the hands of little ones, steer a bike, pull a wagon, take care of a first-aid injury, or handle a flashlight or other piece of gear.

Plan with kids and the elderly in mind

You may be in top physical condition, but if you have babies, young children, sickly or elderly loved ones with you, what then?

When my kids were babies, I would occasionally don a backpack and carry them in a front baby-carrier. I never tried carrying the two for more than a couple of hours, but if this option sounds workable to you, start taking walks around the neighborhood carrying both. It's just a situation like this that calls for your best physical condition.

Don't leave a plan this important to the very last minute when seconds count and you have no idea what to do. Running away and leaving behind someone you dearly love isn't an option.

Transporting kids can be as basic as using a baby carrier as mentioned, a stroller, or a bike trailer or baby bike seat.

Some do's for getting out on foot or bike

DO invest in the best quality bike you can afford and buy several spare inner tubes, a portable pump, a patch kit, and small hand tools for repairs.

DO learn how to change a bike tire and make minor bike repairs yourself. Most bike shops offer this information, and possibly classes, for free.

DO shop around for bike trailers. There are some excellent trailers that are built for rugged wear and tear. Even if you don't have little ones, this is a worthwhile investment if your evacuation plans include possibly going by bike.

DO equip toddlers and young children to walk, with sturdy shoes and comfortable clothing suitable for the weather. Eventually, they'll start to get antsy in that wagon or trailer, so they might as well be prepared to hoof it along with everyone else!

DO spend time carrying your child for lengthy periods of time, around the house, on errands, and on walks around the neighborhood. This will help strengthen your own muscles, your back muscles, in particular, and help your child become accustomed to this very cool mode of transportation!

DO have a baby carrier that can be worn by other members of the family. Older siblings, dad, and other relatives can all take turns.

DO keep comfortable walking shoes, socks, and moleskin stored in your vehicle. You never know when a break-down could happen or, in spite of your best laid plans, you encounter the Mother of All Traffic Jams and have no choice but to hoof it to your destination.

DO keep a bottle of ibuprofen handy. Sooner or later, someone in the family will have a headache, a backache, sore feet, aching shoulders, you name it!

DO have floppy hats for the kids, in particular. A baby sleeping in a stroller or baby carrier is vulnerable to sunburn.

DO put one of the slower adults at the head of the group, whether walking or bicycling, the younger members in the middle, and finally, a strong adult at the rear. The leader can set the pace, the younger members are protected, and the adult bringing up the rear can keep an eye on the whole group and assist when necessary.

In populated areas, DO be prepared for authorities to direct traffic, both pedestrian and otherwise. You may or may not be allowed to venture on to a route other than the one officially designated.

DO take advantage of alternate modes of transportation, if the opportunity presents itself. Depending on your location and the readiness of local emergency personnel, public transportation may be available. If you have a pocketful of change and small bills, you'll be ready.

DO think creatively if you have handicapped or elderly family members. Explore the possibility of using a modern rickshaw or a recumbent bike. The website Bikes at Work has some creative and very heavy duty options for bike trailers.

DO plan on taking frequent breaks, whether walking or bicycling. It's far better to arrive at a destination a couple hours late than to collapse in exhaustion halfway there.

Getting ready to leave: the final moments

One of the hardest parts of evacuation is not knowing how your home will fare while you are gone. In an urgent evacuation, you most likely will not have time to do more than race out and hope for the best. In a planned evacuation, however, there is a lot more you can do to prepare and secure your home for your return.

Here are a few tips:

- **Turn off utilities** such as gas and electricity unless you are expecting freezing temperatures.
- **Prepare for freezing temperatures** if your evacuation occurs in the winter. You don't want to return home to frozen pipes.
  - Drain all outside water lines, including those leading to a swimming pool and a sprinkler system.
  - Turn off water to outside faucets, if possible.
  - Cover outside faucets with anything from a towel or old blanket to a foam outlet cover specially designed for this purpose.
  - Shut off the main water supply and flush all toilets.
  - Insulate all water pipes, both hot and cold,

in unheated or potentially unheated (if the power fails) areas of your home or outbuildings, such as crawl spaces and attics.
- Even several sheets of newspaper wrapped around pipes can protect pipes in areas that are moderately cold.
- In the coldest parts of the country, protect pipes with thermostatically controlled heat tape.
- Disconnect and drain garden hoses and store them for the season. When they freeze, they can increase water pressure throughout the entire plumbing system.
- Leave the gas and electricity connected and set the thermostat no lower than 55 degrees.

- **Board up windows if warranted.** Close all curtains, blinds, and shutters.
- **Make sure all windows and doors are locked.** Be sure to take your house keys with you. Leave one with a trusted neighbor who might be staying behind. They may have to enter your house if flooding or some other emergency occurs.
- **If you're expecting heavy winds,** bring inside patio furniture, trash cans, toys, bicycles, and anything else that might get blown away — or float away, in case of a flood.
- **Disconnect major appliances,** other than the refrigerator and freezers, even if the power is already out. When it comes back on, the surge could damage appliances and electronics.
- **Disconnect computers** and unplug everything else throughout the house.

- **Clean out your refrigerator.** Condiments like ketchup will probably be fine, but items that will spoil easily should be taken with you, tossed, or put in a deep freeze. Unpleasant smells are very difficult to get out of a refrigerator, as liquid from rotting food can drip into the insulation. A chest freezer is worth the risk, especially if it contains a larger amount of frozen foods. Add a few 2-liter bottles filled with water and let them freeze overnight. They'll provide an additional layer of insulation to keep frozen foods cold for as long as possible.
- **Quick check to know if the freezer contents are a loss or not:** Put a bag of ice cubes in the chest freezer before you leave; even a sandwich baggie of them will do. When you return, if the ice cubes are still separate, your freezer is fine. If they have formed a solid block, consider the freezer a loss.

A word about insurance

According to professional emergency managers, there's nothing like having your own private insurance when it comes to recovery and restoration of property following a disaster. It's not recommended that you plan to rely on FEMA or any other type of government help when it comes to getting back on your feet.

FEMA primarily provides disaster assistance to state and local governments, not to families, and even then those loans are given only in major disasters and are based on income level.

Even if you have homeowner's or renter's insurance, set aside some time to review your policy with the company or your agent. It's surprising how quickly our insurance needs change, and it's no fun to find out that your policy doesn't quite cover a new claim.

Ask about flood insurance, no matter where you live. When I lived in Phoenix, smack dab in the middle of the desert, homes would flood on a regular basis due to flash floods. Your homeowner's insurance will cover flooding if it occurs within the house, such as broken pipes. Once the water enters through the outside, however, that damage isn't covered unless you have flood insurance.

Earthquake coverage is another specialty policy you may want to get, especially with earthquakes cropping up in unusual places lately. I never thought of Oklahoma as an earthquake hotspot, but there's a lot of shaking going on in that state!

Use a camera, even if it's just your cell phone camera, to take pictures of every room of the house. Include photos of appliances, walls, and ceilings. You want to document, in detail, the condition of your home and all its contents prior to any damage.

Once damage has occurred, document that also. One insurance expert emphasized to me the importance of having photo documentation, and with cell phone cameras, there's no excuse to not take care of this step.

Your insurance company will provide the best coverage and service by far, over FEMA or any other agency.

If you do experience a major disaster, think Katrina or a devastating earthquake, contact FEMA to find out what assistance you might qualify for.

Rehearsals: practice makes perfect

All your evacuation plans may be in vain if you don't take

EMERGENCY EVACUATIONS

time for a dry-run. If you find yourself in a situation where you must make an immediate and urgent evacuation, you will automatically fall back on behaviors and actions that are familiar and "easy." When you have no time to do anything but react, you need to be sure that your immediate gut reactions are ones that will keep you safe.

In martial arts and self-defense training, this practice is referred to as "muscle memory." A new self-defense technique will not help you if you can't think how to execute it when your life depends on it. The technique must be practiced so many times that you can do it when you're caught off-guard at a moment's notice.

Martial arts instructors aren't the only ones to preach muscle memory. Evacuation rehearsals are a regular fixture of American embassies and military bases throughout the world. These are much more elaborate than your average family evacuation strategy because they tend to involve helicopters, aircraft carriers, and lots and lots of hot dogs.

How can you organize a practice evacuation for your family? Set aside some time one weekend when all family members will be home and no one is busy. Time yourselves to see how long it takes from the moment you announce the evacuation until all supplies are in the car and all family members buckled in.

Before launching this new family experience, create your own Evacuation To Do List based on your own circumstances. You can use the checklist in the Appendix of this book to help you get started.

With the help of your checklist, it's time to have a family meeting to review the plan and the list. Each person should know what to do, even if it's as simple as getting their favorite toy and going outside to sit in their car seat!

Once you've finished your family's evacuation rehearsal, evaluate how long it takes to run through your list. Identify potential problems and create a plan that will help you to smooth out these problems in an event of an actual evacuation. Schedule one of these drills every 60-90 days. That will cover different seasons and weather conditions and will establish a type of muscle memory for family members.

Here is a sample list. You'll find a copy of this checklist in the Appendix that you can customize to your own needs.

Evacuation to-do list

- Each person has on shoes and a jacket.
- Animals in crates
- Pet evacuation kits packed
- Evacuation kits in car
- Grab-n-Go binder in car
- Purses/wallets/cell phones/chargers in car
- Fireproof safes in car – If they are too heavy, leave them behind.
- Suitcases in car — In a planned evacuation you'll have more time to pack additional supplies.
- Water bottles in car — Individual water bottles should already be packed in emergency kits. Add one or two cases of water bottles when evacuating.
- Pack additional personal items and put in car.
- Pack additional clothing items and put in car.
- Pack additional food items and put in car.
- Refer to Last Minute Packing List and make sure those items are packed and in the vehicle.
- Load extra filled containers of gasoline.

- Pack infants and toddlers in their car seats, if temperatures permit. This will allow everyone else to rush around, taking care of last minute details, without worrying about the young ones.

Optional: based on situation and weather conditions

- Turn house water off
- Gas off – Don't do this during a rehearsal! You won't be able to turn your gas on by yourself; it must be done by a representative from the gas company.
- Follow other guidelines found in this chapter to get your house ready, depending on the crisis and current weather conditions.

Final actions

- Load animals in car
- Lock all doors and windows
- Set security alarm
- Contact communications hub and alert him or her to your time of departure, route, and expected arrival time.
- Make sure everyone is in the vehicle

Case study: Hurricane evacuations

There's no way to execute a full-blown city-wide evacuation in the name of rehearsal and it would be crazy to try, but you can still learn from the past and apply lessons learned to future disasters. As I've mentioned, the plan for evacuating the city of Houston during hurricane Rita in 2005 was a disaster. To put it another way, there was no plan.

Evacuees reported that they spent on average twelve

hours on the road. For one family, a trip from Houston to Austin took almost 19 hours when it should have taken just three! There was no way for ambulances to make it through the gridlock to administer relief to those involved in medical emergencies. Many people ran out of gas and had to sleep in their cars on the highway. It was chaos. There was, however, a silver lining: when Hurricane Ike hit Houston in 2008, city officials had a much better idea what they were facing and planned accordingly.

During the evacuation ahead of Hurricane Ike, the city set up emergency pit stop stations with ambulances, portable toilets, and fuel trucks. The city headed an aggressive and effective education campaign to ensure that those outside the danger zones would stay home instead of contributing to traffic. The evacuation was not picture-perfect, but it was a great improvement over the previous attempt.

This lesson is applicable to individual families as well. It is very safe to assume that you will run into problems the first time you evacuate. Therefore, you really don't want the first time you evacuate to be during an actual emergency when emotions are running high and the stakes are even higher.

Even if your emergency kits aren't fully packed and you have no idea, yet, of a destination, schedule a rehearsal anyway. Nearly everything on the Evacuation To Do List can be included in the drill. You will learn so much from the first drill that will help refine your preparations and plans. Be sure to keep track of how much time it takes before everyone and everything is loaded in the car and make a list of everything that goes right, and wrong! Use that information to improve the process, one rehearsal at a time.

EMERGENCY EVACUATIONS

You'll find a copy of this Evacuation To Do List in the Appendix.

Your mindset really matters

This may be the most difficult part of emergency preparedness. You can plan, prepare, and organize until the cows come home, but if you are the kind of person who will panic when things get hairy, all your preparations will be for nothing. You have to train yourself to have a different outlook altogether.

One reason this is vital is that our kids pick up on our emotions, and the only thing worse than Mom or Dad panicking is having a passel of kids also hyperventilating.

In a situation like an emergency evacuation, keep in mind Robert Louis Stevenson's quote, "Share your courage but keep your fears to yourself."

Lots of superhero action movies depict the protagonists doing all kinds of brave and reckless things as if it were all in a day's work. "Sure, I'll just take out seven or eight guys now and then save the city before lunchtime. No big deal."

The implication is that these characters do not feel fear or pain the way normal people do. The implication is also that this is somehow the emotional ideal.

The reality, of course, is that real-life superheroes — first responders, like firefighters, EMTs, and military personnel — face an extraordinary amount of fear when they are called upon to do their jobs. But they have developed the skills to control their emotions instead of being controlled by them. They don't think about what must be done, they do it. Admittedly, this is easier said than done.

Human "wiring"

I could share many amusing anecdotes from horror movies about people who flip out and then die. My favorite example is the guy from *Jurassic Park: The Lost World* who, while trying to hide from a Tyrannosaurus Rex, freaks out when he finds a snake crawling all over him. He blows his cover and immediately, the T-rex eats him. Maybe that snake wasn't even poisonous but because he panicked, he lost his life. Don't be that guy.

We are wired for fight, flight, or freeze in dangerous situations. Freezing can actually be very beneficial in certain dangers (such as that T-rex), but in modern life, we need to learn how to overcome this tendency so we can act when we need to. (If the man had been rational, he would have recognized the T-rex as a greater threat than the snake.) The "wiring" we are born with can make this harder, or easier.

Per a National Institutes of Health study[2], higher anxiety levels before a dangerous event make flight or freezing responses more likely. If you are a person who is a worrier, the best thing you can do to improve your mindset and your ability to respond is to learn how to set worries aside and take action on those you have some control over. If you are naturally an easy-going, no-worries person, staying calm in an emergency will probably be easier for you.

Muscle memory

In an emergency, it is critical to prepare in advance, and that preparation is both physical and mental. This is why it's so important to think through possible emergencies, physically plan for each, and then go through the motions of a rehearsal, or drill, as though the actual emergency was taking place.

As you rehearse the various components of an evacuation, you're not just exercising your brain, but your body is also remembering the motions, tasks, and appropriate reactions. Muscle memory!

If you have practiced taking bicycle routes on your backwoods escape plan, carrying loaded backpacks many times as a family, you will automatically follow the right route and adjust your packs so they don't hurt. If you drive your escape route every time your family takes a trip in that general direction, you will follow it even when you don't intend to. It doesn't matter how simple the item or task, practicing using it during normal life will help lower stress during an emergency because you will know, 100%, that you can do what you need to.

Establishing muscle memory by mentally and physically rehearsing the steps in an evacuation can help take away anxiety.

Anxiety

Sometimes it seems like everyone is anxious today. Even my friend's dog has severe anxiety problems! Anxiety is clearly bad for us and, as noted by National Institutes of Health, it makes our responses worse in an emergency.

John Leach, author of *Survival Psychology*, wrote, "In an emergency, 75% of people have to be told what to do. Only 10-15% of the people act appropriately, leaving the remaining 10-15% sitting on the sidelines acting inappropriately."

Clearly, we need to reduce our anxiety responses. But how?

Part of the answer is being mentally prepared and developing muscle memory, but there is more to it. We need to accept that "bad things" happen all the time and most of them aren't as horrific as the worst-case scenarios our brains create. In the case study below, Beth's son fell in a pool, but didn't have any lasting physical or mental scars. You probably have similar events in your own life. What was it you feared the most, and how did it turn out?

"We have nothing to fear but fear itself" is a good saying to keep in mind. While there may be a great many things to fear in the moment, in the long run, fear seems to cause more problems than anything else, and it certainly doesn't help solve immediate problems. Holding that fear at bay and taking things one step at a time will help you survive and thrive in even the worst situations. And the best way I know to keep that fear at bay is to be prepared – mentally, physically, spiritually, and materially.

A mentor of mine once gave me this great advice, "Lisa, when you're not sure what to do, just do the next thing."

An emergency evacuation, by its nature, is scary and stressful. Initially, it may seem overwhelming to react appropriately. In that case, pause for just a moment and ask yourself, "What is the next thing I should do right now?"

Adopting a mindset that will enable to you to get through the evacuation and then the aftermath of the crisis is crucial. Developing solid muscle memory, being prepared, and learning to conquer your anxiety will go a long way toward developing that critical mindset.

TIP: Let me teach you the 16-Second Survival Breath. This technique has seen me through more than a few scary situations, helping me stay calm and thinking clearly.

Be sure to count to four at each interval.

1. Take four seconds to slowly inhale: 1, 2, 3, 4, taking a slow, deep breath.
2. Hold that breath for four seconds and count 1, 2, 3, 4.
3. Exhale to the count of four, 1, 2, 3, 4.
4. Relax for four seconds before taking the next breath.

I've found that forcing myself to focus on my breathing and counting helps my brain to regain its equilibrium and I'm better able to focus on the crisis at hand.

Case study: Mental preparation

One mom, Beth, told me the story of her son's close encounter with a swimming pool and how she had mentally prepared herself for such an incident in advance.

"When my son was two years old, he fell into a pool. He had never seen one before, and walked around the edge, admiring it. Every few feet, he would bend down, splash his hand in the pool, and get back up again. No fool I, I decided to stay by his side so I would be available should the worst happen. I was not the least surprised when, during his third circuit of the pool, he slipped and fell in. I saw him sink down, down into the pool as if in slow motion.

Without thinking about it, I reached down, grabbed him by

his arm, and pulled him out. He gasped like a fish, his eyes wider than dinner plates, unsure what had just happened. Apart from being shaken and very wet, he was fine. He had been submerged for less than ten seconds. When we went inside and told our family members what had happened, I laughed and joked about it. It wasn't until several hours later, when the shock wore off, that I started shaking with fear, desperately sick at the thought of what might have happened.

Since I could see what was coming, I was mentally and physically prepared (I stayed right beside him, watching closely) and reacted quickly. I did not panic because I had mentally rehearsed what I would do when, or if, he fell in. I didn't have to waste time thinking about what I could do, I simply acted."

Because Beth had already recognized the swimming pool as a potential danger and had given some thought how she might react if her son fell in, her brain kicked into gear, causing her body to do exactly what she had imagined!

LISA BEDFORD

Eventually, you'll return home

Every storm eventually passes and so will whatever event forced you from your home. The question then becomes, what will you come home to?

A house burned to the ground?
Belongings strewn for miles around?
A home or apartment vandalized?

When you return

First, don't be too proud to ask for help! When massive tornadoes hit Joplin, Missouri, in 2011, one friend of mine packed up her kids and headed there, determined to find ways to help complete strangers whose lives had been turned upside down.

Trust me. When you need help the most, there are people just waiting to lend a hand. Don't be too proud to ask.

If you have young children, they will need to be comforted but also kept occupied and distracted. This is the perfect task for an older teenager or another friend to cover while you get in touch with your insurance company, salvage what you can, and take photos for documentation.

Do move quickly to get a rental car or hotel, since these will go quickly as other refugees return.

If your home is damaged but still safe enough for you to

enter, rent a portable storage unit to be delivered to your house. This unit will hold any furniture and other belongings you can salvage in the coming days. PODS is one such company that provides this service. If there's not much to salvage, share the expense of this unit with a neighbor.

Review the contents of your Grab-n-Go binder to refresh your memory of companies and people you need to contact with information about your current status.

Get to work. No matter how shell-shocked you may feel, activity and routine are the best medicine. Sooner than you think, you'll again feel in control of your situation and your life.

Case study: a real-life flood survivor

Ann Johnson, a Survival Mom in Arkansas, tells the story of returning to her home and place of business following a massive flood in 1993, once it was safe to do so:

"I suddenly realized I was homeless with no clothes except the ones on my back. My business was filled with water, and it wasn't covered by flood insurance. Since there had not been a flood in Valley Junction in 100 years, I never thought I needed it.

Once the water receded, I was able to go to my house to clean up. There I was inside, devastated at the loss. I'll never forget it. Paneling on the walls had bent and bulged out like it was hanging there with a thread. I went in the kitchen, and everything was ruined – washer, dryer, small appliances. Dishes covered in mud.

I opened the basement door only to see an ugly river of muddy black water staring back at me. I was in shock. My brother broke open a basement window and was able to pump out the water, but my house would never be the same.

Thanks to the Red Cross and hot meals they provided, I got some cleaning supplies and with energy from their help, I started on clean up. People from several churches came to my rescue in cleaning out a home that I would eventually have to say good-bye to.

One final task was to clean out the garage. Thanks to a wonderful friend who lent me a pair of garden boots, I was able to use a piece of plywood and scrape the muck and mire from the walls and floors. To my horror, a hundred snakes had taken refuge in my garage.

It continued to rain for several days. The day I went up against the snakes in my garage and basement it was raining so hard that when I was finished cleaning, I just stood under the eaves and allowed the fresh rain water to wash away the bad memories

Now homeless, I was able to find a blanket to put over me, and I walked for three blocks in shock looking for help at a nearby church. There, people fed me and led me to a phone bank where I called my son in D.C. The wisdom that came from this 19 year old son was like the balm of Gilead upon my bruised heart. He reminded me that I have Faith and God was still there. He convinced me to call an aunt and uncle, cousins, and nearby friends. They came from all over in groups – family, friends and strangers – to help me rebuild my building and my life.

Churches donated money. Clients helped. The local lumber yard donated everything I could ever need. Bankers came and dry walled the soggy, moldy walls. In fact, folks came from all over the United States when they heard that our little community needed help.

I applied to FEMA for aid two times. I was turned down because they thought I was too poor to pay them back. A wonderful woman banker from my church believed in me and loaned me money, not once but twice. I paid back the money in five years' time.

God was good and eventually, my business was back up and running. I am still a hair dresser in Arkansas after 42 years. I am still thanking God and all the people that came to help me survive the floods of 1993."

Your return will likely not be as traumatic as Ann's, but her story carries a few lessons.

LISA BEDFORD

Prepare more, panic less

There is no place in the world that is completely safe from every conceivable disaster. There is always some known danger that you can prepare for and then those sudden unpleasant surprises that crop up.

For those growing up in coastal regions, hurricanes are a threat. Life in the arid deserts of the southwest can bring long-term drought, flash flooding, and extreme heat waves. On top of that, those unknown disasters could strike at any moment.

This does not mean you now have permission to live in constant fear! Rather, it means that with just a little forethought, you can live with the confidence that your family will be prepared to meet such a disaster should it come. Sometimes an evacuation is simply the prudent course; sometimes it's the only course.

By creating an evacuation plan and then rehearsing it, you will have the peace of mind of knowing that you will be ready to face real danger when, or if, it arrives. This is particularly important in families. As the saying goes, "If the generals don't panic, the troops won't panic." A pre-determined plan that everyone is familiar with will alleviate panic and dissipate fear.

With all the pieces in place, you'll be ready to lead your

EMERGENCY EVACUATIONS

family to safety without chaos or panic. Prepare more, panic less.

Acknowledgements

No book is an island. Every book's author has been surrounded by supportive people, from family to friends and colleagues who have helped make its creation possible.

This book was no exception.

My assistant, Bethanne Kim, has provided excellent editorial help, honest opinions, and has been staunchly loyal to The Survival Mom brand almost from its inception.

Joyce Richardson lent a hand with her invaluable proofreading assistance.

Inspiration, real life anecdotes, and checklist help was provided by Beth Buck and Amy Van Riper, just two of the truly excellent contributing writers to my blog.

I also want to thank the Survival Moms who shared their stories with me.

Finally, to my wonderful family, Stephen, Olivia, and Andrew, who give me more support and love than I probably deserve, thank you. xoxoxo

EMERGENCY EVACUATIONS

Appendixes

EMERGENCY EVACUATIONS

Evacuation supplies checklist

Sustenance

All of these foods and beverages are shelf-stable and typically do very well in varying temperatures. Be sure to have a can opener.

- ☐ Can opener – One per family.
- ☐ Utensils – One set per person. (Plastic is fine.)
- ☐ Small cup and plate – One per person.
- ☐ Water bottle or canteen – One per person.
- ☐ Hard candies
- ☐ 5 days' worth of food
- ☐ Energy bars (high calorie)
- ☐ Powdered energy drink mix
- ☐ V-8 juice
- ☐ Gatorade mix
- ☐ Cocoa or hot apple cider mixes
- ☐ Instant coffee, if ya just gotta have it!
- ☐ Packets of dry milk
- ☐ Shelf stable milk
- ☐ Just-add-hot-water freeze dried meals
- ☐ MRE's (heat sensitive)
- ☐ Ready-to-eat canned meals, such as chili and beef stew
- ☐ Breakfast bars
- ☐ Almonds and other nuts
- ☐ Sunflower seeds
- ☐ Granola
- ☐ Canned pasta
- ☐ Tuna packs
- ☐ Peanut butter or other nut butter
- ☐ Jerky

EMERGENCY EVACUATIONS

- ☐ Dried fruit/fruit leather
- ☐ Canned fruit
- ☐ Applesauce/fruit cups
- ☐ Rice cakes
- ☐ Pilot bread
- ☐ Triscuits or other hard cracker
- ☐ Crackers
- ☐ Cheese spread in jars
- ☐ Cookies
- ☐ Pudding cups

Sanitation supplies

- ☐ Flattened roll of toilet paper or a packet or 2 of tissues
- ☐ Bar of soap in a plastic box with lid
- ☐ Feminine hygiene products, if necessary
- ☐ Wet wipes/diaper wipes
- ☐ Hand sanitizer
- ☐ Toothbrush
- ☐ Toothpaste
- ☐ Dental floss
- ☐ Change of clothes
- ☐ Small hand towel
- ☐ Shampoo
- ☐ A roll of dog poop bags for waste disposal (or zip-locs!)

Sanity

- ☐ Small notebook
- ☐ Pencil and pencil sharpener
- ☐ Foam ear plugs
- ☐ Deck of cards
- ☐ Books on CD

- ☐ Sharpie marker
- ☐ Age-appropriate entertainment items
- ☐ Bible or other inspirational book

Security

- ☐ Firearm
- ☐ Loaded magazines
- ☐ Bear spray
- ☐ Pepper spray
- ☐ Emergency phone numbers and addresses
- ☐ Cell phone charger
- ☐ Cash – Enough to cover expenses for at least 5 days, including hotel, gas, and food.

Survival

- ☐ A portable radio – One per family.
- ☐ A first aid kit – A few basics packed in each kit, a larger kit in the family emergency bag
- ☐ Prescription medication
- ☐ Over-the-counter medication
- ☐ Waterproof matches or lighter – Teens and adults only.
- ☐ Fire starters
- ☐ Flashlight or other light source
- ☐ Extra batteries
- ☐ Emergency blanket
- ☐ Rain poncho
- ☐ Duct tape
- ☐ Paracord
- ☐ Whistle
- ☐ Maps of area
- ☐ Laminated map of immediate area with marked

EMERGENCY EVACUATIONS

    evacuation routes
- [ ] Tarp
- [ ] Portable water filter
- [ ] Pocket knife and/or multi-tool
- [ ] Thumb drive with scanned documents, family photos, and other important information
- [ ] Cotton, brimmed hat
- [ ] Work gloves
- [ ] Hand/foot warmers
- [ ] Heavy duty trash bags
- [ ] Sunblock
- [ ] Insect repellent

Evacuation to-do list

- ☐ Each person has shoes on and a jacket
- ☐ Animals in crates
- ☐ Pet evacuation/emergency kit in car
- ☐ All evacuation kits in car
- ☐ Grab-n-Go binder in car
- ☐ Purses/wallets/cell phones/chargers in car
- ☐ Fireproof safes in car
- ☐ Additional suitcases or bags in car
- ☐ Laptops/chargers in car
- ☐ Cases of water bottles in car
- ☐ Pack additional personal items and put in car.
- ☐ Pack additional clothing items and put in car.
- ☐ Pack additional food items and put in car.
- ☐ Refer to Last Minute Packing List and make sure those items are packed and in the vehicle.
- ☐ Load extra filled containers of gasoline.
- ☐ Pack infants and toddlers in car seats
- ☐ _____
- ☐ _____
- ☐ _____

Optional: based on situation & weather conditions

- ☐ Turn house water off
- ☐ Turn gas off
- ☐ Turn off electricity
- ☐ _____
- ☐ _____
- ☐ _____

EMERGENCY EVACUATIONS

Final Actions

- ☐ Load animals in car
- ☐ Lock all doors and windows
- ☐ Set security alarm
- ☐ Contact communications hub and alert him or her to your time of departure, route, and expected arrival time.
- ☐ All people in car
- ☐ _____
- ☐ _____
- ☐ _____

Last-minute packing list

- ☐ Cash – Include locations of each stash!
     Example: $250/desk drawer.

  _____
  _____
  _____

- ☐ Medications – List each one and location.
     Example: Adderall/hall bathroom.

  _____
  _____
  _____
  _____

- ☐ Medical equipment

  _____
  _____
  _____

- ☐ Supplies/equipment for special needs family member

  _____
  _____
  _____

- ☐ Firearms, magazines, ammunition, and related supplies

  _____
  _____

- ☐ Cold/rainy weather clothing and shoes

  _____
  _____

EMERGENCY EVACUATIONS

- ☐ Heirlooms and other valuables (list)
  _____
  _____
  _____

- ☐ Photo albums or files (if not already stored and ready to pack)
  _____
  _____
  _____

- ☐ Strong box/safes
  _____
  _____

- ☐ Kindle or other e-book reader and chargers
  _____
  _____

- ☐ Electronics that cannot be left behind
  _____
  _____
  _____

- ☐ Grab-n-Go binder
  _____

- ☐ Perishable foods
  _____
  _____

- ☐ Ice chest
  _____
  _____

☐ Comfort items

_____
_____
_____

☐ Family pets and their supplies

_____
_____

☐ Camping supplies

_____
_____
_____

☐ School textbooks, assignments, and supplies

_____
_____
_____

Footnotes

[1]Shashi Shekhar, McKnight Distinguished University Professor, University of Minnesota Director, Army High Performance Computing Research Center. Evacuation Route Planning: A Scientific Approach, University of Minnesota, Minneapolis, Minnesota, (April 2006)

[2]"Exploring Human Freeze Responses to a Threat Stressor" "Ewww.ncbi.nlm.nih.gov/pmc/articles/PMC2489204/

Afterword

Because Amazon reviews really do matter, please take a few minutes and post a review on Amazon.com.

Thank you in advance for writing a quick and honest review of this book.

And...

If you want to learn more about these and many more preparedness topics, sign up for my email at http://forms.aweber.com/form/73/1863723773.htm

About the author

LISA BEDFORD is better known to millions around the world as The Survival Mom, a preparedness-minded author, blogger, and keynote speaker who encourages families to adopt a calm and common-sense approach to an uncertain future.

When she started her blog, The Survival Mom, in 2009, very little attention was given to women in the survival and prepper world. She changed all that with her friendly, sound advice, understanding that, above all, moms want to keep their homes and families safe and secure.

Lisa has been featured in *Newsweek*, on the *Glenn Beck* show and *The Today Show,* and in countless interviews in magazines, newspapers, radio shows, and podcasts.

She is the author of *Survival Mom: How to Prepare Your Family For Everyday Disasters and Worst Case Scenarios*, an Amazon #1 bestseller published by Harper Collins.

She believes there's power and peace in being prepared and draws from her 25 years of experience as a teacher, trainer, and world traveler to carry that message to others through her writing, classes, webinars, and speaking engagements.

Also by Lisa Bedford

Survival Mom: How to Prepare Your Family for Everyday Disasters and Worst Case Scenarios

Undaunted by the prospect of TEOTWAWKI (The End of the World as We Know It), Lisa Bedford tackles every what-if and worst-case scenario head-on, offering practical advice on how to prepare your family for whatever might come your way. From a few days without electricity to an unexpected job loss or total chaos after the destruction of a tornado, Survival Mom provides everything you need to become self-reliant and establish plans for your family, including:

- Preparing the home for a natural disaster.
- Alternative sources of energy in a power's-out situation.
- Everything you need to know about food storage.
- Personal protection. (Do I really need to learn how to shoot a gun?)

Deep inside every mom is a Survival Mom whose passion for her family drives her to make the best of the present and prepare for the future. So tap into your Mama Grizzly

EMERGENCY EVACUATIONS

instincts and channel your worries into action. Whether you're a full-fledged "prepper" or just getting started, with real-life stories and customizable forms and checklists along with Lisa's "you can do it" attitude, Survival Mom replaces paranoia and panic with the peace of knowing YOU have the power to keep your loved ones safe and secure.

Available on Amazon, Barnes & Noble, and through your local bookstores.

Happy, Healthy, and Prepared: Top Tips From the Hosts of The Survival Mom Radio Network

Edited by Lisa Bedford

The Survival Mom Radio Network is an online resource of more than 700 recorded podcast episodes from over a dozen amazing women hosts, experts in all areas of preparedness. This handy e-book includes their very best top tips for preserving food, frugal living, survival skills, gardening tips, and more. Enjoy this FREE e-book as my gift to you, a fellow Survival Mom! Available through Amazon, Barnes & Noble, and other e-book retailers.

Forthcoming:

Watch for this new title in the Survival Mom's No Worries Guide series:

101 Best Survival Tips

Have you ever wondered just how many "survival tips" can be found on the internet? A Google search turns up more than 90 million different pages!

The Survival Mom, Lisa Bedford, has combed through her own website, with more than 1700 articles, and has selected 101 of the very best tips for moms and families. In this upcoming book she includes:

- ✓ Unusual items to add to your survival supplies
- ✓ A snoop-free foreign language
- ✓ Her favorite grocery store for food storage bargains
- ✓ The best discount coupons for prepping
- ✓ Camping must-haves for non-campers
- ✓ ...and 96 more!

Watch for this new release coming in early 2016!

Contact the author.

You can connect with Lisa Bedford through:

Her blog – http://thesurvivalmom.com/

Via email – Lisa@TheSurvivalMom.com

On Facebook – The-Survival-Mom

Follow her on Pinterest – TheSurvivalMom

On Twitter – TheSurvivalMom

Made in the USA
San Bernardino, CA
15 December 2015